Microsoft® Outloo

ILLUSTRATED

Essentials

Microsoft® Outlook® 2010

ILLUSTRATED

Essentials

Rachel Biheller Bunin

COURSE TECHNOLOGY
CENGAGE Learning™

Australia • Brazil • Japan • Korea • Mexico • Singapore • Spain • United Kingdom • United States

COURSE TECHNOLOGY
CENGAGE Learning™

Microsoft® Outlook® 2010—Essentials

Rachel Biheller Bunin

Vice President, Publisher: Nicole Jones Pinard

Executive Editor: Marjorie Hunt

Associate Acquisitions Editor: Brandi Shailer

Senior Product Manager: Christina Kling Garrett

Associate Product Manager: Michelle Camisa

Editorial Assistant: Kim Klasner

Director of Marketing: Cheryl Costantini

Senior Marketing Manager: Ryan DeGrote

Marketing Coordinator: Kristen Panciocco

Contributing Authors: Carol Cram, Elizabeth Eisner Reding

Developmental Editors: Barbara Clemens, Pamela Conrad, Jeanne Herring

Content Project Manager: Heather Hopkins

Copy Editor: John Bosco and Mark Goodin

Proofreader: Harold Johnson

Indexer: BIM Indexing and Proofreading Services

QA Manuscript Reviewers: John Frietas, Jeff Schwartz, Susan Whalen

Print Buyer: Fola Orekoya

Cover Designer: GEX Publishing Services

Cover Artist: Mark Hunt

Composition: GEX Publishing Services

For product information and technology assistance, contact us at
Cengage Learning Customer & Sales Support, 1-800-354-9706
For permission to use material from this text or product, submit all requests online at **www.cengage.com/permissions**
Further permissions questions can be emailed to
permissionrequest@cengage.com

Trademarks:

Some of the product names and company names used in this book have been used for identification purposes only and may be trademarks or registered trademarks of their respective manufacturers and sellers.

Microsoft and the Office logo are either registered trademarks or trademarks of Microsoft Corporation in the United States and/or other countries. Course Technology, Cengage Learning is an independent entity from Microsoft Corporation, and not affiliated with Microsoft in any manner.

Library of Congress Control Number: 2010931916

ISBN-13: 978-0-538-74925-1

ISBN-10: 0-538-74925-3

Course Technology
20 Channel Center Street
Boston, MA 02210
USA

Cengage Learning is a leading provider of customized learning solutions with office locations around the globe, including Singapore, the United Kingdom, Australia, Mexico, Brazil, and Japan. Locate your local office at:
international.cengage.com/region

Cengage Learning products are represented in Canada by Nelson Education, Ltd.

To learn more about Course Technology, visit **www.cengage.com/coursetechnology**

To learn more about Cengage Learning, visit **www.cengage.com**

Purchase any of our products at your local college store or at our preferred online store
www.cengagebrain.com

Printed in the United States of America
1 2 3 4 5 6 7 8 9 18 17 16 15 14 13 12 11 10

Brief Contents

Contents

Preface

Welcome to *Microsoft Outlook® 2010—Illustrated Essentials*. If this is your first experience with the Illustrated series, you'll see that this book has a unique design: each skill is presented on two facing pages, with steps on the left and screens on the right. The layout makes it easy to learn a skill without having to read a lot of text and flip pages to see an illustration.

This book is an ideal learning tool for a wide range of learners—the "rookies" will find the clean design easy to follow and focused with only essential information presented, and the "hotshots" will appreciate being able to move quickly through the lessons to find the information they need without reading a lot of text. The design also makes this a great reference after the course is over! See the illustration on the right to learn more about the pedagogical and design elements of a typical lesson.

About This Edition

- **Fully Updated.** Updated examples and exercises throughout highlight the features of Microsoft Outlook 2010 including sending and receiving e-mail, organizing contacts, managing appointments, tracking tasks, creating notes, and using the journal. New Appendix covers cloud computing concepts and using Microsoft Office Web Apps.

- **Maps to SAM 2010.** This book is designed to work with SAM (Skills Assessment Manager) 2010. **SAM Assessment** contains performance-based, hands-on SAM exams, and **SAM Training** provides hands-on training to enhance retention of skills covered in the book. (SAM sold separately.) See page xii for more information on SAM.

Each two-page spread focuses on a single skill.

Introduction briefly explains why the lesson skill is important.

A case scenario motivates the the steps and puts learning in context.

UNIT
B

Outlook 2010

Adding Contacts

Contacts in Microsoft Outlook let you manage all your business and personal contact information. When you create a contact for a person with whom you want to communicate, you store general and detailed information about that person in fields. A **field** is an area that stores one piece of information, such as a first name or an e-mail address. Once you create a contact, you can quickly address letters, locate a phone number, make a call, send a meeting request, assign a task, or e-mail a message. You can sort, group, and filter contacts by any field. You can also easily share contacts with others. You learn about Contacts so you can store all the contact information for employees and clients in Outlook.

STEPS

QUICK TIP
Click the Normal or Cards Only buttons on the status bar to change the view. Use the Zoom slider to increase or decrease the size and number of cards that fit on a screen.

1. Click Contacts in the Navigation Pane, click the View tab, click the To-Do Bar button in the Layout group, then click Off
   The Navigation Pane changes to Contacts view, and the To-Do Bar closes. Figure B-8 shows several completed contacts in a Contacts folder in Business Card view.

2. Click the Home tab, then click the New Contact button in the New group
   You enter information for a new contact in each field in the Contact window.

3. Type your name as the contact name in the Full Name text box, press [Tab], type Quest Specialty Travel (QST) in the Company text box, press [Tab], type Human Resources Assistant in the Job title text box, then type your E-mail address, Business, Home, and Mobile telephone numbers in the appropriate text boxes
   If you do not enter a first and last name in the Full Name text box, the Check Full Name dialog box opens so you can enter the full name for the contact. Determine how Outlook files each contact by clicking the File as list arrow in the Contact window, then click by first name, last name, company, or job title.

TROUBLE
If the Location Information dialog box opens, enter your local area code, click OK, then click OK in the Phone and Modem dialog box.

4. Click the Addresses list arrow, click Business if necessary, click the This is the mailing address check box to select it if necessary, then type your address in the Address text box
   You can store up to three addresses in the Address text box. Choose Business, Home, or Other from the Addresses list, then type the address in the Address text box. If Outlook can't identify an address component that you type in the Address text box, the Check Address dialog box opens for you to verify the component.

5. Click the MapIt button in the Contact card
   If your computer is connected to the Internet, a browser window opens and shows the location on a map.

6. Close the browser window if it is open, click the Business Card button in the Options group to open the Edit Business Card dialog box, click Full Name, Company, Job Title, Business Phone, and Business Address in the Fields list to view the information for each field in the Edit window on the right, then click Cancel
   You use the Edit Business Card dialog box to view and edit, when necessary, contact information.

7. Click the Picture button in the Options group, then click Add Picture
   You use the Add Contact Picture dialog box to navigate to select the photo, and then click Open.

QUICK TIP
When you create a new Outlook item, such as a task, appointment, or note, you can link it to the contact or contacts to which it relates.

8. Add a photo if you have one, or click Cancel, then click the Details button in the Show group on the Contact card
   You can enter a contact's detailed information, including the contact's department, profession, assistant's name, birthday, anniversary, spouse or partner's name, or even the contact's nickname.

9. Click the Click to Expand the People Pane button in the Contact card, view the Social Networking options, click the Click to collapse the People Pane button in the People Pane, then click the Save & Close button in the Actions group
   Figure B-9 shows a Contact card with a photo as a business card.

Outlook 30   Managing Information Using Outlook

Tips and troubleshooting advice, right where you need it–next to the step itself.

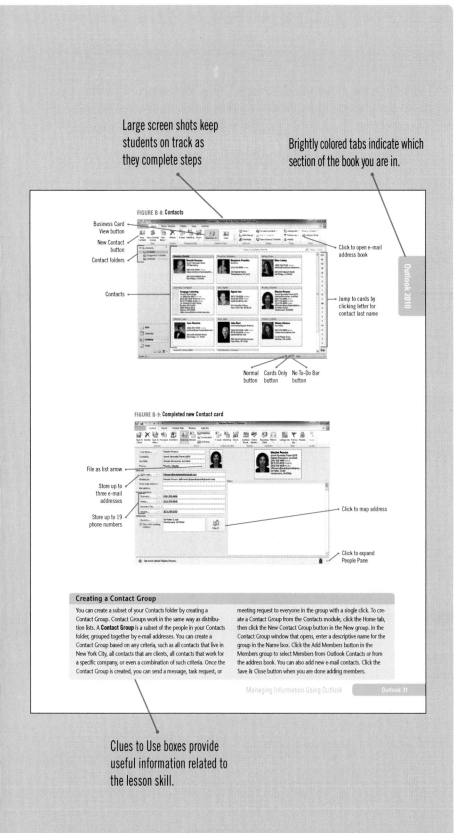

Large screen shots keep students on track as they complete steps

Brightly colored tabs indicate which section of the book you are in.

FIGURE B-8: Contacts

Business Card View button
New Contact button
Contact folders
Contacts

Click to open e-mail address book

Jump to cards by clicking letter for contact last name

Normal button
Cards Only button
No To-Do Bar button

Outlook 2010

FIGURE B-9: Completed new Contact card

File as list arrow
Store up to three e-mail addresses
Store up to 19 phone numbers

Click to map address

Click to expand People Pane

Creating a Contact Group

You can create a subset of your Contacts folder by creating a Contact Group. Contact Groups work in the same way as distribution lists. A **Contact Group** is a subset of the people in your Contacts folder, grouped together by e-mail addresses. You can create a Contact Group based on any criteria, such as all contacts that live in New York City, all contacts that are clients, all contacts that work for a specific company, or even a combination of such criteria. Once the Contact Group is created, you can send a message, task request, or meeting request to everyone in the group with a single click. To create a Contact Group from the Contacts module, click the Home tab, then click the New Contact Group button in the New group. In the Contact Group window that opens, enter a descriptive name for the group in the Name box. Click the Add Members button in the Members group to select Members from Outlook Contacts or from the address book. You can also add new e-mail contacts. Click the Save & Close button when you are done adding members.

Clues to Use boxes provide useful information related to the lesson skill.

Assignments

The lessons use Quest Specialty Travel, a fictional adventure travel company, as the case study. The assignments on the light yellow pages at the end of each unit increase in difficulty. Assignments include:

- **Concepts Review** consist of multiple choice, matching, and screen identification questions.

- **Skills Reviews** are hands-on, step-by-step exercises that review the skills covered in each lesson in the unit.

- **Independent Challenges** are case projects requiring critical thinking and application of the unit skills. The Independent Challenges increase in difficulty, with the first one in each unit being the easiest. Independent Challenges 2 and 3 become increasingly open-ended, requiring more independent problem solving.

- **Real Life Independent Challenges** are practical exercises in which students create documents to help them with their every day lives.

- **Advanced Challenge Exercises** set within the Independent Challenges provide optional steps for more advanced students.

- **Visual Workshops** are practical, self-graded capstone projects that require independent problem solving.

About SAM

SAM is the premier proficiency-based assessment and training environment for Microsoft Office. Web-based software along with an inviting user interface provide maximum teaching and learning flexibility. SAM builds students' skills and confidence with a variety of real-life simulations, and SAM Projects' assignments prepare students for today's workplace.

The SAM system includes Assessment, Training, and Projects, featuring page references and remediation for this book as well as Course Technology's Microsoft Office textbooks. With SAM, instructors can enjoy the flexibility of creating assignments based on content from their favorite Microsoft Office books or based on specific course objectives. Instructors appreciate the scheduling and reporting options that have made SAM the market-leading online testing and training software for over a decade. Over 2,000 performance-based questions and matching Training simulations, as well as tens of thousands of objective-based questions from many Course Technology texts, provide instructors with a variety of choices across multiple applications from the introductory level through the comprehensive level. The inclusion of hands-on Projects guarantee that student knowledge will skyrocket from the practice of solving real-world situations using Microsoft Office software.

SAM Assessment

- Content for these hands-on, performance-based tasks includes Word, Excel, Access, PowerPoint, Internet Explorer, Outlook, and Windows. Includes tens of thousands of objective-based questions from many Course Technology texts.

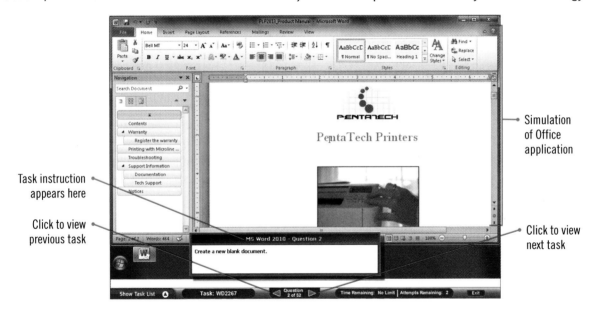

SAM Training

- Observe mode allows the student to watch and listen to a task as it is being completed.
- Practice mode allows the student to follow guided arrows and hear audio prompts to help visual learners know how to complete a task.
- Apply mode allows the student to prove what they've learned by completing a task using helpful instructions.

SAM Projects

- Live-in-the-application assignments in Word, Excel, Access and PowerPoint that help students be sure they know how to effectively communicate, solve a problem or make a decision.
- Students receive detailed feedback on their project within minutes.
- Additionally, teaches proper file management techniques.
- Ensures that academic integrity is not compromised, with unique anti-cheating detection encrypted into the data files.

Instructor Resources

The Instructor Resources CD is Course Technology's way of putting the resources and information needed to teach and learn effectively into your hands. With an integrated array of teaching and learning tools that offer you and your students a broad range of technology-based instructional options, we believe this CD represents the highest quality and most cutting edge resources available to instructors today. The resources available with this book are:

- **Instructor's Manual**—Available as an electronic file, the Instructor's Manual includes detailed lecture topics with teaching tips for each unit.

- **Sample Syllabus**—Prepare and customize your course easily using this sample course outline.

- **PowerPoint Presentations**—Each unit has a corresponding PowerPoint presentation that you can use in lecture, distribute to your students, or customize to suit your course.

- **Figure Files**—The figures in the text are provided on the Instructor Resources CD to help you illustrate key topics or concepts. You can create traditional overhead transparencies by printing the figure files. Or you can create electronic slide shows by using the figures in a presentation program such as PowerPoint.

- **Solutions to Exercises**—Solutions to Exercises contains every file students are asked to create or modify in the lessons and end-of-unit material. Also provided in this section, there is a document outlining the solutions for the end-of-unit Concepts Review, Skills Review, and Independent Challenges. An Annotated Solution File and Grading Rubric accompany each file and can be used together for quick and easy grading.

- **Data Files for Students**—To complete most of the units in this book, your students will need Data Files. You can post the Data Files on a file server for students to copy. The Data Files are available on the Instructor Resources CD-ROM, the Review Pack, and can also be downloaded from cengagebrain.com. For more information on how to download the Data Files, see the inside back cover.

Instruct students to use the Data Files List included on the Review Pack and the Instructor Resources CD. This list gives instructions on copying and organizing files.

- **ExamView**—ExamView is a powerful testing software package that allows you to create and administer printed, computer (LAN-based), and Internet exams. ExamView includes hundreds of questions that correspond to the topics covered in this text, enabling students to generate detailed study guides that include page references for further review. The computer-based and Internet testing components allow students to take exams at their computers, and also saves you time by grading each exam automatically.

Content for Online Learning.

Course Technology has partnered with the leading distance learning solution providers and class-management platforms today. To access this material, visit www.cengage.com/webtutor and search for your title. Instructor resources include the following: additional case projects, sample syllabi, PowerPoint presentations, and more. For additional information, please contact your sales representative. For students to access this material, they must have purchased a WebTutor PIN-code specific to this title and your campus platform. The resources for students might include (based on instructor preferences): topic reviews, review questions, practice tests, and more.

Acknowledgements

Instructor Advisory Board

We thank our Instructor Advisory Board who gave us their opinions and guided our decisions as we updated our texts for Microsoft Office 2010. They are as follows:

Terri Helfand, Chaffey Community College

Barbara Comfort, J. Sargeant Reynolds Community College

Brenda Nielsen, Mesa Community College

Sharon Cotman, Thomas Nelson Community College

Marian Meyer, Central New Mexico Community College

Audrey Styer, Morton College

Richard Alexander, Heald College

Xiaodong Qiao, Heald College

Student Advisory Board

We also thank our Student Advisory Board members, who shared their experiences using the Illustrated Series and offered suggestions to make it better: **Latasha Jefferson**, Thomas Nelson Community College, **Gary Williams**, Thomas Nelson Community College, **Stephanie Miller**, J. Sargeant Reynolds Community College, **Sarah Styer**, Morton Community College, **Missy Marino**, Chaffey College

Author Acknowledgements

Rachel Biheller Bunin Thank you to Marjorie Hunt, Christina Kling Garrett, and Heather Hopkins at Cengage Learning for their hard work and for making this book possible. Appreciation to my awesome colleague and development editor, Barbara Clemens, for her keen eye and wonderful suggestions. My special thanks to David, Jennifer, Emily, and Michael.

Read This Before You Begin

Frequently Asked Questions

What are Data Files?

A Data File is a partially completed Word document, Excel workbook, Access database, PowerPoint Presentation, or another type of file that you use to complete the steps in the units and exercises to create the final document that you submit to your instructor. Each unit opener page lists the Data Files that you need for that unit.

Where are the Data Files?

Your instructor will provide the Data Files to you or direct you to a location on a network drive from which you can download them. For information on how to download the Data Files from cengagebrain.com, see the inside back cover.

What software was used to write and test this book?

This book was written and tested using a typical installation of Microsoft Office 2010 Professional Plus on a computer with a typical installation of Microsoft Windows 7 Ultimate.

The browser used for any Web-dependent steps is Internet Explorer 8.

Do I need to be connected to the Internet to complete the steps and exercises in this book?

Some of the exercises in this book require that your computer be connected to the Internet. If you are not connected to the Internet, see your instructor for information on how to complete the exercises.

What do I do if my screen is different from the figures shown in this book?

This book was written and tested on computers with monitors set at a resolution of 1024 × 768. If your screen shows more or less information than the figures in the book, your monitor is probably set at a higher or lower resolution. If you don't see something on your screen, you might have to scroll down or up to see the object identified in the figures.

The Ribbon—the blue area at the top of the screen—in Microsoft Office 2010 adapts to different resolutions. If your monitor is set at a lower resolution than 1024 × 768, you might not see all of the buttons shown in the figures. The groups of buttons will always appear, but the entire group might be condensed into a single button that you need to click to access the buttons described in the instructions.

COURSECASTS **Learning on the Go. Always Available...Always Relevant.**

Our fast-paced world is driven by technology. You know because you are an active participant—always on the go, always keeping up with technological trends, and always learning new ways to embrace technology to power your life. Let CourseCasts, hosted by Ken Baldauf of Florida State University, be your guide into weekly updates in this ever-changing space. These timely, relevant podcasts are produced weekly and are available for download at http://coursecasts.course.com or directly from iTunes (search by CourseCasts). CourseCasts are a perfect solution to getting students (and even instructors) to learn on the go!

UNIT A
Office 2010

Getting Started with Microsoft Office 2010

Files You Will Need:

OFFICE A-1.xlsx

Microsoft Office 2010 is a group of software programs designed to help you create documents, collaborate with coworkers, and track and analyze information. Each program is designed so you can work quickly and efficiently to create professional-looking results. You use different Office programs to accomplish specific tasks, such as writing a letter or producing a sales presentation, yet all the programs have a similar look and feel. Once you become familiar with one program, you'll find it easy to transfer your knowledge to the others. This unit introduces you to the most frequently used programs in Office, as well as common features they all share.

OBJECTIVES

Understand the Office 2010 suite

Start and exit an Office program

View the Office 2010 user interface

Create and save a file

Open a file and save it with a new name

View and print your work

Get Help and close a file

Understanding the Office 2010 Suite

Microsoft Office 2010 features an intuitive, context-sensitive user interface, so you can get up to speed faster and use advanced features with greater ease. The programs in Office are bundled together in a group called a **suite** (although you can also purchase them separately). The Office suite is available in several configurations, but all include Word, Excel, and PowerPoint. Other configurations include Access, Outlook, Publisher, and other programs. Each program in Office is best suited for completing specific types of tasks, though there is some overlap in capabilities.

DETAILS

The Office programs covered in this book include:

- **Microsoft Word 2010**

  When you need to create any kind of text-based document, such as a memo, newsletter, or multipage report, Word is the program to use. You can easily make your documents look great by inserting eye-catching graphics and using formatting tools such as themes, which are available in most Office programs. **Themes** are predesigned combinations of color and formatting attributes you can apply to a document. The Word document shown in Figure A-1 was formatted with the Solstice theme.

- **Microsoft Excel 2010**

  Excel is the perfect solution when you need to work with numeric values and make calculations. It puts the power of formulas, functions, charts, and other analytical tools into the hands of every user, so you can analyze sales projections, calculate loan payments, and present your findings in style. The Excel worksheet shown in Figure A-1 tracks personal expenses. Because Excel automatically recalculates results whenever a value changes, the information is always up to date. A chart illustrates how the monthly expenses are broken down.

- **Microsoft PowerPoint 2010**

  Using PowerPoint, it's easy to create powerful presentations complete with graphics, transitions, and even a soundtrack. Using professionally designed themes and clip art, you can quickly and easily create dynamic slide shows such as the one shown in Figure A-1.

- **Microsoft Access 2010**

  Access helps you keep track of large amounts of quantitative data, such as product inventories or employee records. The form shown in Figure A-1 was created for a grocery store inventory database. Employees use the form to enter data about each item. Using Access enables employees to quickly find specific information such as price and quantity without hunting through store shelves and stockrooms.

Microsoft Office has benefits beyond the power of each program, including:

- **Common user interface: Improving business processes**

  Because the Office suite programs have a similar **interface**, or look and feel, your experience using one program's tools makes it easy to learn those in the other programs. In addition, Office documents are **compatible** with one another, meaning that you can easily incorporate, or **integrate**, an Excel chart into a PowerPoint slide, or an Access table into a Word document.

- **Collaboration: Simplifying how people work together**

  Office recognizes the way people do business today, and supports the emphasis on communication and knowledge sharing within companies and across the globe. All Office programs include the capability to incorporate feedback—called **online collaboration**—across the Internet or a company network.

FIGURE A-1: Microsoft Office 2010 documents

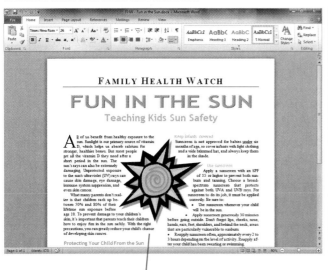

Newsletter created in Word

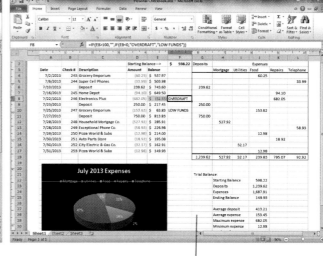

Checkbook register created in Excel

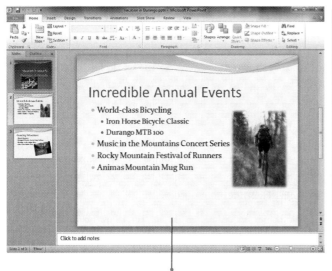

Tourism presentation created in PowerPoint

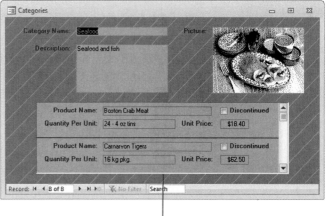

Store inventory form created in Access

Deciding which program to use

Every Office program includes tools that go far beyond what you might expect. For example, although Excel is primarily designed for making calculations, you can use it to create a database. So when you're planning a project, how do you decide which Office program to use? The general rule of thumb is to use the program best suited for your intended task, and make use of supporting tools in the program if you need them. Word is best for creating text-based documents, Excel is best for making mathematical calculations, PowerPoint is best for preparing presentations, and Access is best for managing quantitative data. Although the capabilities of Office are so vast that you *could* create an inventory in Excel or a budget in Word, you'll find greater flexibility and efficiency by using the program designed for the task. And remember, you can always create a file in one program, and then insert it in a document in another program when you need to, such as including sales projections (Excel) in a memo (Word).

Starting and Exiting an Office Program

The first step in using an Office program is to open, or **launch**, it on your computer. The easiest ways to launch a program are to click the Start button on the Windows taskbar or to double-click an icon on your desktop. You can have multiple programs open on your computer simultaneously, and you can move between open programs by clicking the desired program or document button on the taskbar or by using the [Alt][Tab] keyboard shortcut combination. When working, you'll often want to open multiple programs in Office and switch among them as you work. Begin by launching a few Office programs now.

STEPS

1. **Click the Start button 🌑 on the taskbar**

   The Start menu opens. If the taskbar is hidden, you can display it by pointing to the bottom of the screen. Depending on your taskbar property settings, the taskbar may be displayed at all times, or only when you point to that area of the screen. For more information, or to change your taskbar properties, consult your instructor or technical support person.

2. **Click All Programs, scroll down if necessary in the All Programs menu, click Microsoft Office as shown in Figure A-2, then click Microsoft Word 2010**

   Word 2010 starts, and the program window opens on your screen.

3. **Click 🌑 on the taskbar, click All Programs, click Microsoft Office, then click Microsoft Excel 2010**

   Excel 2010 starts, and the program window opens, as shown in Figure A-3. Word is no longer visible, but it remains open. The taskbar displays a button for each open program and document. Because this Excel document is **active**, or in front and available, the Excel button on the taskbar appears slightly lighter.

4. **Point to the Word program button 🅦 on the taskbar, then click 🅦**

   The Word program window is now in front. When the Aero feature is turned on in Windows 7, pointing to a program button on the taskbar displays a thumbnail version of each open window in that program above the program button. Clicking a program button on the taskbar activates that program and the most recently active document. Clicking a thumbnail of a document activates that document.

5. **Click 🌑 on the taskbar, click All Programs, click Microsoft Office, then click Microsoft PowerPoint 2010**

   PowerPoint 2010 starts and becomes the active program.

6. **Click the Excel program button 🅧 on the taskbar**

   Excel is now the active program.

7. **Click 🌑 on the taskbar, click All Programs, click Microsoft Office, then click Microsoft Access 2010**

   Access 2010 starts and becomes the active program. Now all four Office programs are open at the same time.

8. **Click Exit on the navigation bar in the Access program window, as shown in Figure A-4**

   Access closes, leaving Excel active and Word and PowerPoint open.

Using shortcut keys to move between Office programs

As an alternative to the Windows taskbar, you can use a keyboard shortcut to move among open Office programs. The [Alt][Tab] keyboard combination lets you either switch quickly to the next open program or file or choose one from a gallery. To switch immediately to the next open program or file, press [Alt][Tab]. To choose from all open programs and files, press and hold [Alt], then press and release [Tab] without releasing [Alt]. A gallery opens on screen, displaying the filename and a thumbnail image of each open program and file, as well as of the desktop. Each time you press [Tab] while holding [Alt], the selection cycles to the next open file or location. Release [Alt] when the program, file, or location you want to activate is selected.

FIGURE A-2: **Start menu**

All programs menu (yours will look different)

Start button   Taskbar

FIGURE A-3: **Excel program window and Windows taskbar**

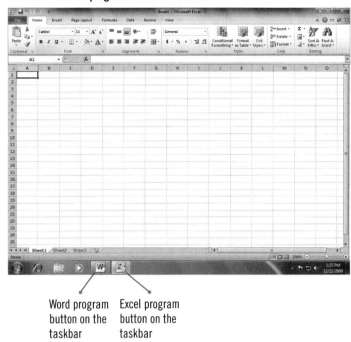

Word program button on the taskbar

Excel program button on the taskbar

FIGURE A-4: **Access program window**

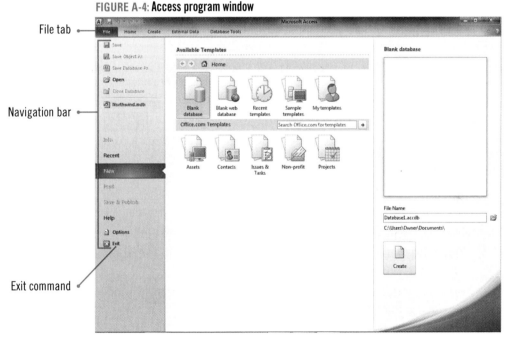

File tab

Navigation bar

Exit command

Windows Live and Microsoft Office Web Apps

All Office programs include the capability to incorporate feedback—called online collaboration—across the Internet or a company network. Using **cloud computing** (work done in a virtual environment), you can take advantage of Web programs called Microsoft Office Web Apps, which are simplified versions of the programs found in the Microsoft Office 2010 suite. Because these programs are online, they take up no computer disk space and are accessed using

Windows Live SkyDrive, a free service from Microsoft. Using Windows Live SkyDrive, you and your colleagues can create and store documents in a "cloud" and make the documents available to whomever you grant access. To use Windows Live SkyDrive, you need a free Windows Live ID, which you obtain at the Windows Live Web site. You can find more information in the "Working with Windows Live and Office Web Apps" appendix.

Viewing the Office 2010 User Interface

One of the benefits of using Office is that the programs have much in common, making them easy to learn and making it simple to move from one to another. Individual Office programs have always shared many features, but the innovations in the Office 2010 user interface mean even greater similarity among them all. That means you can also use your knowledge of one program to get up to speed in another. A **user interface** is a collective term for all the ways you interact with a software program. The user interface in Office 2010 provides intuitive ways to choose commands, work with files, and navigate in the program window. Familiarize yourself with some of the common interface elements in Office by examining the PowerPoint program window.

1. **Click the PowerPoint program button on the taskbar**

   PowerPoint becomes the active program. Refer to Figure A-5 to identify common elements of the Office user interface. The **document window** occupies most of the screen. In PowerPoint, a blank slide appears in the document window, so you can build your slide show. At the top of every Office program window is a **title bar** that displays the document name and program name. Below the title bar is the **Ribbon**, which displays commands you're likely to need for the current task. Commands are organized onto **tabs**. The tab names appear at the top of the Ribbon, and the active tab appears in front. The Ribbon in every Office program includes tabs specific to the program, but all Office programs include a File tab and Home tab on the left end of the Ribbon.

2. **Click the File tab**

   The File tab opens, displaying **Backstage view**. The navigation bar on the left side of Backstage view contains commands to perform actions common to most Office programs, such as opening a file, saving a file, and closing the current program. Just above the File tab is the **Quick Access toolbar**, which also includes buttons for common Office commands.

3. **Click the File tab again to close Backstage view and return to the document window, then click the Design tab on the Ribbon**

   To display a different tab, you click the tab on the Ribbon. Each tab contains related commands arranged into **groups** to make features easy to find. On the Design tab, the Themes group displays available design themes in a **gallery**, or visual collection of choices you can browse. Many groups contain a **dialog box launcher**, an icon you can click to open a dialog box or task pane from which to choose related commands.

4. **Move the mouse pointer over the Angles theme in the Themes group as shown in Figure A-6, but do not click the mouse button**

   The Angles theme is temporarily applied to the slide in the document window. However, because you did not click the theme, you did not permanently change the slide. With the **Live Preview** feature, you can point to a choice, see the results right in the document, and then decide if you want to make the change.

5. **Move away from the Ribbon and towards the slide**

   If you had clicked the Angles theme, it would be applied to this slide. Instead, the slide remains unchanged.

6. **Point to the Zoom slider on the status bar, then drag to the right until the Zoom level reads 166%**

   The slide display is enlarged. Zoom tools are located on the status bar. You can drag the slider or click the Zoom In or Zoom Out buttons to zoom in or out on an area of interest. **Zooming in**, or choosing a higher percentage, makes a document appear bigger on screen, but less of it fits on the screen at once; **zooming out**, or choosing a lower percentage, lets you see more of the document but at a reduced size.

7. **Drag on the status bar to the left until the Zoom level reads 73%**

FIGURE A-5: PowerPoint program window

Quick Access toolbar

Ribbon

Clipboard dialog box launcher

Title bar

Tabs

Document window

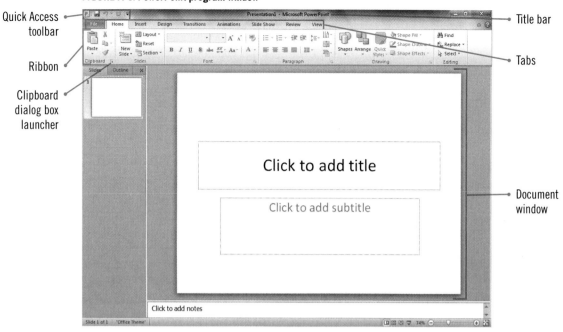

FIGURE A-6: Viewing a theme with Live Preview

Angles theme

Mouse pointer

Live Preview of Angles theme applied to document

Zoom slider

Zoom In button

Zoom level

Zoom Out button

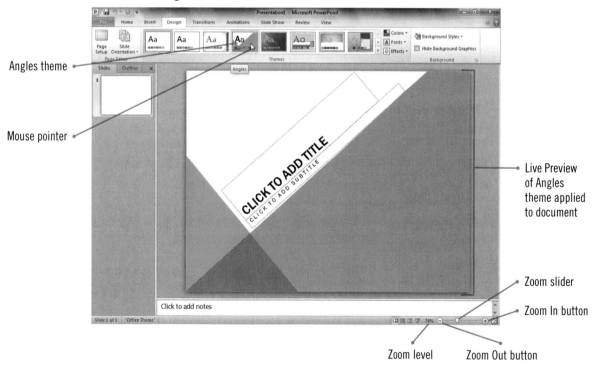

Using Backstage view

Backstage view in each Microsoft Office program offers "one stop shopping" for many commonly performed tasks, such as opening and saving a file, printing and previewing a document, defining document properties, sharing information, and exiting a program.

Backstage view opens when you click the File tab in any Office program, and while features such as the Ribbon, Mini toolbar, and Live Preview all help you work *in* your documents, the File tab and Backstage view help you work *with* your documents.

Creating and Saving a File

When working in a program, one of the first things you need to do is to create and save a file. A **file** is a stored collection of data. Saving a file enables you to work on a project now, then put it away and work on it again later. In some Office programs, including Word, Excel, and PowerPoint, a new file is automatically created when you start the program, so all you have to do is enter some data and save it. In Access, you must expressly create a file before you enter any data. You should give your files meaningful names and save them in an appropriate location so that they're easy to find. ▓▓▓▓▓ Use Word to familiarize yourself with the process of creating and saving a document. First you'll type some notes about a possible location for a corporate meeting, then you'll save the information for later use.

STEPS

1. **Click the Word program button [W] on the taskbar**

2. **Type Locations for Corporate Meeting, then press [Enter] twice**

   The text appears in the document window, and the **insertion point** blinks on a new blank line. The insertion point indicates where the next typed text will appear.

3. **Type Las Vegas, NV, press [Enter], type Orlando, FL, press [Enter], type Boston, MA, press [Enter] twice, then type your name**

   Compare your document to Figure A-7.

   > **QUICK TIP**
   > A filename can be up to 255 characters, including a file extension, and can include upper- or lowercase characters and spaces, but not ?, ", /, \, <, >, *, |, or :.

4. **Click the Save button [icon] on the Quick Access toolbar**

   Because this is the first time you are saving this document, the Save As dialog box opens, as shown in Figure A-8. The Save As dialog box includes options for assigning a filename and storage location. Once you save a file for the first time, clicking [icon] saves any changes to the file *without* opening the Save As dialog box, because no additional information is needed. The Address bar in the Save As dialog box displays the default location for saving the file, but you can change it to any location. The File name field contains a suggested name for the document based on text in the file, but you can enter a different name.

5. **Type OF A-Potential Corporate Meeting Locations**

   The text you type replaces the highlighted text. (The "OF A-" in the filename indicates that the file is created in Office Unit A. You will see similar designations throughout this book when files are named. For example, a file named in Excel Unit B would begin with "EX B-".)

   > **QUICK TIP**
   > Saving a file to the Desktop creates a desktop icon that you can double-click to both launch a program and open a document.

6. **In the Save As dialog box, use the Address bar or Navigation Pane to navigate to the drive and folder where you store your Data Files**

   Many students store files on a flash drive, but you can also store files on your computer, a network drive, or any storage device indicated by your instructor or technical support person.

   > **QUICK TIP**
   > To create a new blank file when a file is open, click the File tab, click New on the navigation bar, then click Create near the bottom of the document preview pane.

7. **Click Save**

   The Save As dialog box closes, the new file is saved to the location you specified, then the name of the document appears in the title bar, as shown in Figure A-9. (You may or may not see the file extension ".docx" after the filename.) See Table A-1 for a description of the different types of files you create in Office, and the file extensions associated with each.

TABLE A-1: Common filenames and default file extensions

file created in	is called a	and has the default extension
Word	document	.docx
Excel	workbook	.xlsx
PowerPoint	presentation	.pptx
Access	database	.accdb

FIGURE A-7: Document created in Word

Save button

Your name should appear here

Insertion point

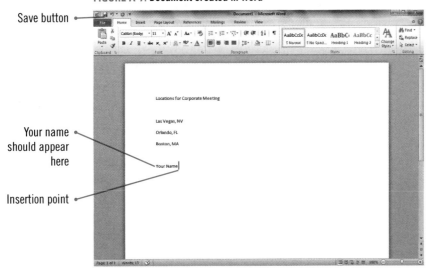

FIGURE A-8: Save As dialog box

Navigation Pane; your links and folders may differ

File name field; your computer may not display file extensions

Address bar

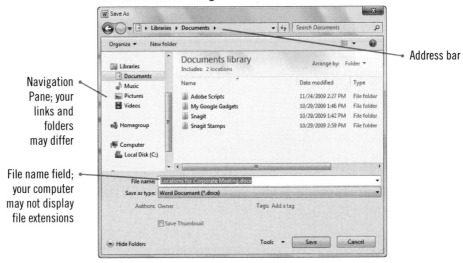

FIGURE A-9: Saved and named Word document

Filename appears in title bar

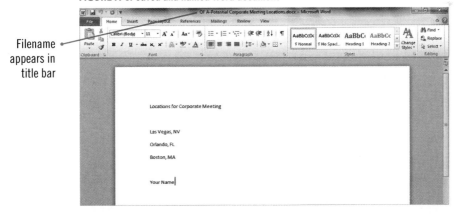

Using the Office Clipboard

You can use the Office Clipboard to cut and copy items from one Office program and paste them into others. The Office Clipboard can store a maximum of 24 items. To access it, open the Office Clipboard task pane by clicking the dialog box launcher ▣ in the Clipboard group on the Home tab. Each time you copy a selection, it is saved in the Office Clipboard. Each entry in the Office Clipboard includes an icon that tells you the program it was created in. To paste an entry, click in the document where you want it to appear, then click the item in the Office Clipboard. To delete an item from the Office Clipboard, right-click the item, then click Delete.

Opening a File and Saving It with a New Name

In many cases as you work in Office, you start with a blank document, but often you need to use an existing file. It might be a file you or a coworker created earlier as a work in progress, or it could be a complete document that you want to use as the basis for another. For example, you might want to create a budget for this year using the budget you created last year; you could type in all the categories and information from scratch, or you could open last year's budget, save it with a new name, and just make changes to update it for the current year. By opening the existing file and saving it with the Save As command, you create a duplicate that you can modify to your heart's content, while the original file remains intact. ▓▓▓▓▓ Use Excel to open an existing workbook file, and save it with a new name so the original remains unchanged.

STEPS

> **QUICK TIP**
> Click Recent on the navigation bar to display a list of recent workbooks; click a file in the list to open it.

1. **Click the Excel program button 🖾 on the taskbar, click the File tab, then click Open on the navigation bar**

   The Open dialog box opens, where you can navigate to any drive or folder accessible to your computer to locate a file.

2. **In the Open dialog box, navigate to the drive and folder where you store your Data Files**

   The files available in the current folder are listed, as shown in Figure A-10. This folder contains one file.

> **TROUBLE**
> Click Enable Editing on the Protected View bar near the top of your document window if prompted.

3. **Click OFFICE A-1.xlsx, then click Open**

   The dialog box closes, and the file opens in Excel. An Excel file is an electronic spreadsheet, so it looks different from a Word document or a PowerPoint slide.

4. **Click the File tab, then click Save As on the navigation bar**

   The Save As dialog box opens, and the current filename is highlighted in the File name text box. Using the Save As command enables you to create a copy of the current, existing file with a new name. This action preserves the original file and creates a new file that you can modify.

> **QUICK TIP**
> The Save As command works identically in all Office programs, except Access; in Access, this command lets you save a copy of the current database object, such as a table or form, with a new name, but not a copy of the entire database.

5. **Navigate to the drive and folder where you store your Data Files if necessary, type OF A-Budget for Corporate Meeting in the File name text box, as shown in Figure A-11, then click Save**

   A copy of the existing workbook is created with the new name. The original file, Office A-1.xlsx, closes automatically.

6. **Click cell A19, type your name, then press [Enter], as shown in Figure A-12**

   In Excel, you enter data in cells, which are formed by the intersection of a row and a column. Cell A19 is at the intersection of column A and row 19. When you press [Enter], the cell pointer moves to cell A20.

7. **Click the Save button 🖫 on the Quick Access toolbar**

   Your name appears in the workbook, and your changes to the file are saved.

Working in Compatibility Mode

Not everyone upgrades to the newest version of Office. As a general rule, new software versions are **backward compatible**, meaning that documents saved by an older version can be read by newer software. To open documents created in older Office versions, Office 2010 includes a feature called Compatibility Mode. When you use Office 2010 to open a file created in an earlier version of Office, "Compatibility Mode" appears in the title bar, letting you know the file was created in an earlier but usable version of the program. If you are working with someone who may not be using the newest version of the software, you can avoid possible incompatibility problems by saving your file in another, earlier format. To do this in an Office program, click the File tab, click Save As on the navigation bar, click the Save as type list arrow in the Save As dialog box, then click an option on the list. For example, if you're working in Excel, click Excel 97-2003 Workbook format in the Save as type list to save an Excel file so that it can be opened in Excel 97 or Excel 2003.

FIGURE A-10: **Open dialog box**

Available files
in this folder

Open button

Open list
arrow

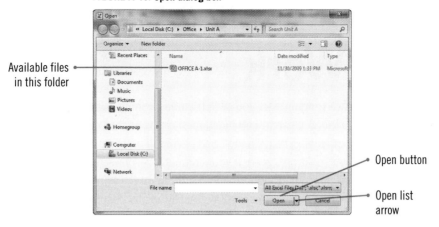

FIGURE A-11: **Save As dialog box**

New filename

Save as type
list arrow

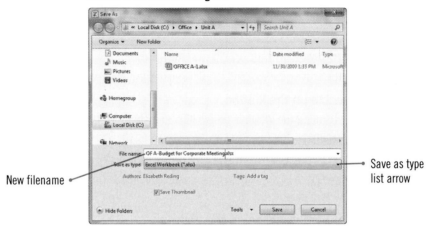

FIGURE A-12: **Your name added to the workbook**

Address for cell A19
formed by column A
and row 19

Cell A19; type
your name here

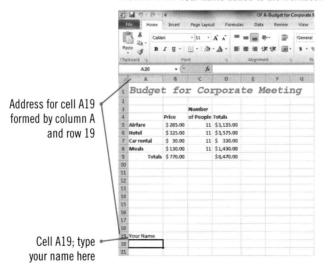

Exploring File Open options

You might have noticed that the Open button on the Open dialog box includes an arrow. In a dialog box, if a button includes an arrow you can click the button to invoke the command, or you can click the arrow to choose from a list of related commands. The Open list arrow includes several related commands, including Open Read-Only and Open as Copy. Clicking Open Read-Only opens a file that you can only save with a new name; you cannot save changes to the original file. Clicking Open as Copy creates a copy of the file already saved and named with the word "Copy" in the title. Like the Save As command, these commands provide additional ways to use copies of existing files while ensuring that original files do not get changed by mistake.

Viewing and Printing Your Work

Each Microsoft Office program lets you switch among various **views** of the document window to show more or fewer details or a different combination of elements that make it easier to complete certain tasks, such as formatting or reading text. Changing your view of a document does not affect the file in any way, it affects only the way it looks on screen. If your computer is connected to a printer or a print server, you can easily print any Office document using the Print button on the Print tab in Backstage view. Printing can be as simple as **previewing** the document to see exactly what a document will look like when it is printed and then clicking the Print button. Or, you can customize the print job by printing only selected pages or making other choices. Experiment with changing your view of a Word document, and then preview and print your work.

STEPS

1. **Click the Word program button [W] on the taskbar**
   Word becomes the active program, and the document fills the screen.

2. **Click the View tab on the Ribbon**
   In most Office programs, the View tab on the Ribbon includes groups and commands for changing your view of the current document. You can also change views using the View buttons on the status bar.

3. **Click the Web Layout button in the Document Views group on the View tab**
   The view changes to Web Layout view, as shown in Figure A-13. This view shows how the document will look if you save it as a Web page.

4. **Click the Print Layout button on the View tab**
   You return to Print Layout view, the default view in Word.

5. **Click the File tab, then click Print on the navigation bar**
   The Print tab opens in Backstage view. The preview pane on the right side of the window automatically displays a preview of how your document will look when printed, showing the entire page on screen at once. Compare your screen to Figure A-14. Options in the Settings section enable you to change settings such as margins, orientation, and paper size before printing. To change a setting, click it, and then click the new setting you want. For instance, to change from Letter paper size to Legal, click Letter in the Settings section, then click Legal on the menu that opens. The document preview is updated as you change the settings. You also can use the Settings section to change which pages to print and even the number of pages you print on each sheet of printed paper. If you have multiple printers from which to choose, you can change from one installed printer to another by clicking the current printer in the Printer section, then clicking the name of the installed printer you want to use. The Print section contains the Print button and also enables you to select the number of copies of the document to print.

6. **Click the Print button in the Print section**
   A copy of the document prints, and Backstage view closes.

> **QUICK TIP**
> You can add the Quick Print button [icon] to the Quick Access toolbar by clicking the Customize Quick Access Toolbar button, then clicking Quick Print. The Quick Print button prints one copy of your document using the default settings.

Customizing the Quick Access toolbar

You can customize the Quick Access toolbar to display your favorite commands. To do so, click the Customize Quick Access Toolbar button [icon] in the title bar, then click the command you want to add. If you don't see the command in the list, click More Commands to open the Quick Access Toolbar tab of the current program's Options dialog box. In the Options dialog box, use the Choose commands from list to choose a category, click the desired command in the list on the left, click Add to add it to the Quick Access toolbar, then click OK. To remove a button from the toolbar, click the name in the list on the right in the Options dialog box, then click Remove. To add a command to the Quick Access toolbar on the fly, simply right-click the button on the Ribbon, then click Add to Quick Access Toolbar on the shortcut menu. To move the Quick Access toolbar below the Ribbon, click the Customize Quick Access Toolbar button, and then click Show Below the Ribbon.

FIGURE A-13: Web Layout view

Web Layout button

View buttons on status bar

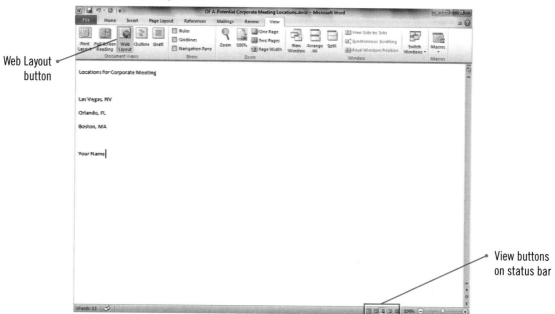

FIGURE A-14: Print tab in Backstage view

Print button

Click to select a different installed printer

Settings section

Preview of document

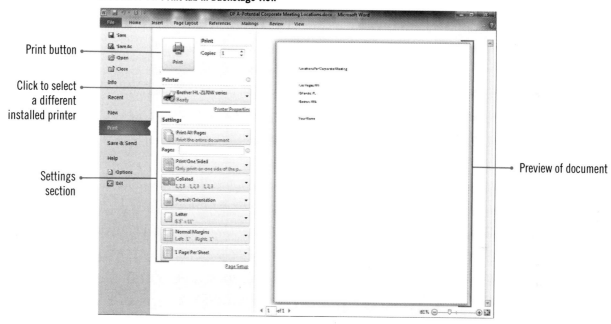

Creating a screen capture

A **screen capture** is a digital image of your screen, as if you took a picture of it with a camera. For instance, you might want to take a screen capture if an error message occurs and you want Technical Support to see exactly what's on the screen. You can create a screen capture using features found in Windows 7 or Office 2010. Windows 7 comes with the Snipping Tool, a separate program designed to capture whole screens or portions of screens. To open the Snipping Tool, click it on the Start menu or click All Programs, click Accessories, then click Snipping Tool. After opening the Snipping Tool, drag the pointer on the screen to select the area of the screen you want to capture. When you release the mouse button, the screen capture opens in the Snipping Tool window, and

you can save, copy, or send it in an e-mail. In Word, Excel, and PowerPoint 2010, you can capture screens or portions of screens and insert them in the current document using the Screenshot button on the Insert tab. And finally, you can create a screen capture by pressing [PrtScn]. (Keyboards differ, but you may find the [PrtScn] button in or near your keyboard's function keys.) Pressing this key places a digital image of your screen in the Windows temporary storage area known as the **Clipboard**. Open the document where you want the screen capture to appear, click the Home tab on the Ribbon (if necessary), then click the Paste button on the Home tab. The screen capture is pasted into the document.

Getting Help and Closing a File

You can get comprehensive help at any time by pressing [F1] in an Office program. You can also get help in the form of a ScreenTip by pointing to almost any icon in the program window. When you're finished working in an Office document, you have a few choices regarding ending your work session. You can close a file or exit a program by using the File tab or by clicking a button on the title bar. Closing a file leaves a program running, while exiting a program closes all the open files in that program as well as the program itself. In all cases, Office reminds you if you try to close a file or exit a program and your document contains unsaved changes. Explore the Help system in Microsoft Office, and then close your documents and exit any open programs.

TROUBLE

If the Table of Contents pane doesn't appear on the left in the Help window, click the Show Table of Contents button on the Help toolbar to show it.

1. **Point to the Zoom button on the View tab of the Ribbon**

   A ScreenTip appears that describes how the Zoom button works and explains where to find other zoom controls.

2. **Press [F1]**

   The Word Help window opens, as shown in Figure A-15, displaying the home page for help in Word on the right and the Table of Contents pane on the left. In both panes of the Help window, each entry is a hyperlink you can click to open a list of related topics. The Help window also includes a toolbar of useful Help commands and a Search field. The connection status at the bottom of the Help window indicates that the connection to Office.com is active. Office.com supplements the help content available on your computer with a wide variety of up-to-date topics, templates, and training. If you are not connected to the Internet, the Help window displays only the help content available on your computer.

QUICK TIP

You can also open the Help window by clicking the Microsoft Office Word Help button to the right of the tabs on the Ribbon.

3. **Click the Creating documents link in the Table of Contents pane**

   The icon next to Creating documents changes, and a list of subtopics expands beneath the topic.

4. **Click the Create a document link in the subtopics list in the Table of Contents pane**

   The topic opens in the right pane of the Help window, as shown in Figure A-16.

QUICK TIP

You can print the entire current topic by clicking the Print button on the Help toolbar, then clicking Print in the Print dialog box.

5. **Click Delete a document under "What do you want to do?" in the right pane**

   The link leads to information about deleting a document.

6. **Click the Accessibility link in the Table of Contents pane, click the Accessibility features in Word link, read the information in the right pane, then click the Help window Close button**

7. **Click the File tab, then click Close on the navigation bar; if a dialog box opens asking whether you want to save your changes, click Save**

   The Potential Corporate Meeting Locations document closes, leaving the Word program open.

8. **Click the File tab, then click Exit on the navigation bar**

   Word closes, and the Excel program window is active.

9. **Click the File tab, click Exit on the navigation bar to exit Excel, click the PowerPoint program button on the taskbar if necessary, click the File tab, then click Exit on the navigation bar to exit PowerPoint**

   Excel and PowerPoint both close.

FIGURE A-15: **Word Help window**

Help toolbar

Search field

The colors of
your links may
differ if the
links have
been visited
previously

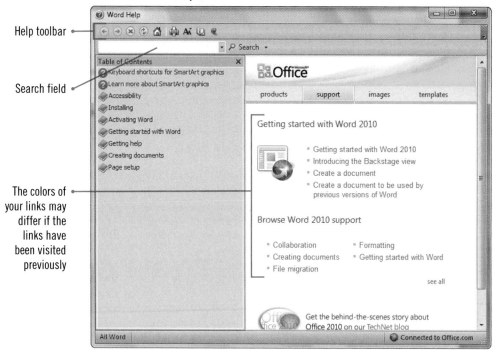

FIGURE A-16: **Create a document Help topic**

Print button

Icon indicates
expanded topic

Create a
document link

Create a
document
topic

Click to read
how to perform
the action
described

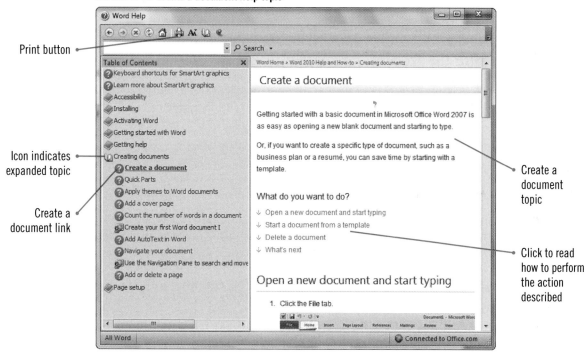

Recovering a document

Each Office program has a built-in recovery feature that allows you to open and save files that were open at the time of an interruption such as a power failure. When you restart the program(s) after an interruption, the Document Recovery task pane opens on the left side of your screen displaying both original and recovered versions of the files that were open. If you're not sure which file to open (original or recovered), it's usually better to open the recovered file because it will contain the latest information. You can, however, open and review all versions of the file that were recovered and save the best one. Each file listed in the Document Recovery task pane displays a list arrow with options that allow you to open the file, save it as is, delete it, or show repairs made to it during recovery.

Practice

Concepts Review

For current SAM information, including versions and content details, visit SAM Central (http://www.cengage.com/samcentral). If you have a SAM user profile, you may have access to hands-on instruction, practice, and assessment of the skills covered in this unit. Since various versions of SAM are supported throughout the life of this text, check with your instructor for the correct instructions and URL/Web site for accessing assignments.

Label the elements of the program window shown in Figure A-17.

FIGURE A-17

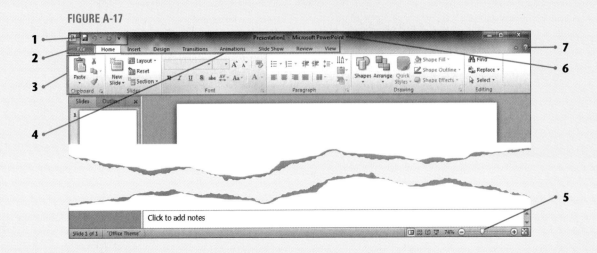

Match each project with the program for which it is best suited.

8. Microsoft Access   a. Corporate convention budget with expense projections
9. Microsoft Excel   b. Business cover letter for a job application
10. Microsoft Word   c. Department store inventory
11. Microsoft PowerPoint   d. Presentation for city council meeting

Independent Challenge 1

You just accepted an administrative position with a local independently owned produce vendor that has recently invested in computers and is now considering purchasing Microsoft Office for the company. You are asked to propose ways Office might help the business. You produce your document in Word.

a. Start Word, then save the document as **OF A-Microsoft Office Document** in the drive and folder where you store your Data Files.
b. Type **Microsoft Word**, press [Enter] twice, type **Microsoft Excel**, press [Enter] twice, type **Microsoft PowerPoint**, press [Enter] twice, type **Microsoft Access**, press [Enter] twice, then type your name.
c. Click the line beneath each program name, type at least two tasks suited to that program (each separated by a comma), then press [Enter].

Advanced Challenge Exercise

- Press the [PrtScn] button to create a screen capture.
- Click after your name, press [Enter] to move to a blank line below your name, then click the Paste button in the Clipboard group on the Home tab.

d. Save the document, then submit your work to your instructor as directed.
e. Exit Word.

Getting Started with E-Mail

Files You Will Need:

Leave No Trace.docx
Bridge.jpg

E-mail is an essential communication tool for business and personal correspondence. You can use a desktop information management program like Microsoft Outlook 2010, an e-mail program, or any of several Web-based e-mail programs to send and receive e-mail. Once you learn the basic features of e-mail, you will be able to use Outlook or any other e-mail program to manage your e-mail. 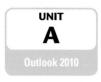 You are an assistant to Juan Ramirez, the personnel director at Quest Specialty Travel (QST). The company uses e-mail for much of its correspondence. Juan wants you to learn the basics of e-mail for your job.

OBJECTIVES

Communicate with e-mail

Compile an e-mail address book

Create and send a message

Manage e-mail folders

Receive and reply to a message

Forward a message

Send a message with an attachment

Employ good e-mail practices

Communicating with E-Mail

Electronic mail (e-mail) is the technology that lets you send and receive written messages through the Internet. The messages sent using e-mail technology are known as **e-mail messages**, or **e-mail** for short. **E-mail software**, such as Microsoft Outlook, shown in Figure A-1, enables you to send and receive e-mail messages over a network, over an intranet, and over the Internet. A **computer network** is the hardware and software that enables two or more computers to share information and resources. An **intranet** is a computer network that connects computers in a local area only, such as computers in a company's office. The **Internet** is a network of connected computers and computer networks located around the world. Quest Specialty Travel employees use e-mail to communicate with each other and with clients around the world because it is fast, reliable, and easy.

DETAILS

E-mail enables you to:

QUICK TIP

E-mail uses store-and-forward technology. Messages are *stored* on a service provider's computer until a recipient logs on to a computer and requests his or her messages. At that time, the messages are *forwarded* to the recipient's computer.

- **Communicate conveniently and efficiently**
  E-mail is an effective way to correspond with coworkers or colleagues. E-mail can be sent from one person to another person or to a group of people anywhere in the world. You can send and receive messages directly from any computer with an Internet or network connection. You can also send and receive e-mail from wireless devices such as smartphones or handheld computers with e-mail capability. Unlike mail sent using the postal service, e-mail is delivered almost instantaneously. Unlike instant messaging recipients, e-mail recipients do not have to be at their computers at the same time that a message is sent in order to receive the message.

- **Send images, video, and documents as well as text information**
  Messages can be formatted so that they are easy to read and appear professional and attractive. Messages can include graphics in the body of the message to convey visual information. In addition, you can attach files to a message, such as a sound or video, photographs, graphics, spreadsheets, or word-processing documents.

- **Communicate with numerous people at once; never forget an address**
  You can create your own electronic address book that stores the names and e-mail addresses of people with whom you frequently communicate. You can send the same message to more than one person at one time. You can also create named groups of e-mail addresses and then send messages to that group of people by entering only the group name.

- **Ensure the delivery of information**
  With e-mail software, you have the option of receiving a delivery confirmation message when a recipient receives your e-mail. In addition, if you are away and unable to access e-mail because of a vacation or other plans, you can set up an automatic message that is delivered to senders so they are alerted to the fact that you might not receive your e-mail for a specified time period.

- **Correspond from a remote place**
  If you have an Internet connection and communications software, you can use your computer or handheld device to send and receive messages from any location. You sign up with an **ISP (Internet service provider)** to send and receive e-mail. If you are using a Web-based e-mail program, like those shown in Figures A-2 and A-3, you can access your e-mail from any computer that is connected to the Internet from anywhere in the world. You can connect to the Internet using a telephone line or use other, faster technologies, including satellite, DSL (digital subscriber line), cable, fiber optic, ISDN (Integrated Services Digital Network), T1, or T3.

- **Organize a record of your communications**
  You can organize the messages you send and receive in a way that best suits your working style. You can store e-mail messages in folders and refer to them again in the future. Organizing your saved messages lets you keep a record of communications to manage a project or business. You can also flag or categorize messages to give an instant visual cue that distinguishes messages that require immediate attention from those that can wait. You can download e-mail to your computer or keep it on the provider's Web server.

FIGURE A-1: Microsoft Outlook

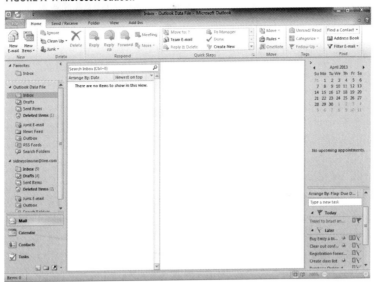

FIGURE A-2: Web-based e-mail: Gmail

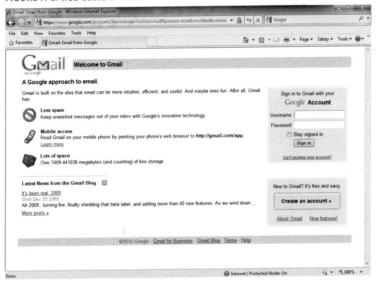

FIGURE A-3: Web-based e-mail: Hotmail

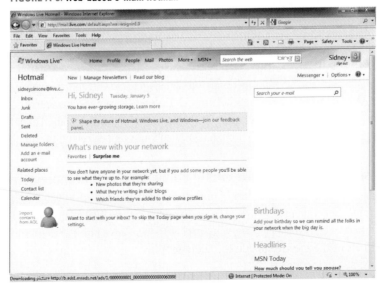

Compiling an E-Mail Address Book

E-mail can be sent from one person to another person or a group of people anywhere in the world. To send and receive e-mail over the Internet using an e-mail program, you must have an e-mail address. Each person has his or her own e-mail address and a password that lets him or her log in to an e-mail program and receive e-mail. To send an e-mail message, you need to know the e-mail address of the person to whom you are sending the message. Instead of having to remember the address of someone to whom you are sending an e-mail, you can select the name you want from an **address book**, a stored list of names and e-mail addresses. At Quest Specialty Travel, each employee is assigned an e-mail address. As the assistant to the personnel director in the Human Resources department, you maintain a list of all employee e-mail addresses in an electronic address book that you use to distribute information about company policies and events through e-mail. You review the parts of an e-mail address and the benefits of maintaining an e-mail address book.

DETAILS

An e-mail address has three parts:

* **Username**

  The first part of an e-mail address is the username. The **username** identifies the person who receives the e-mail sent to the e-mail address. At Quest Specialty Travel, as in many companies, universities, or organizations, usernames are assigned and are based on a specified format. At QST, a username is the first initial of the person's first name and his or her last name. In many e-mail systems, such as those used primarily for personal e-mail, you get to create your username, combining letters and numbers to create a unique username.

* **@ sign**

  The middle part of an e-mail address is the @ sign, called an "at sign." It separates the username from the service provider or e-mail provider name. Every e-mail address includes an @ sign.

QUICK TIP
A person can have more than one e-mail address.

* **Service provider or e-mail provider**

  The last part of the e-mail address is the service provider or e-mail provider. There are many different service providers. For example, the service provider might be the name of the company that a person works for or the name of the school that a person attends. The service provider generally is a company or organization that provides the connection to the Internet and provides e-mail. The service provider can also be the Web site name for a Web-based e-mail program. Table A-1 provides some examples of e-mail address formats that are used with different service providers.

The benefits of an e-mail address book include the following:

* **Stores the names and e-mail addresses of people to whom you send e-mail messages**

  Outlook 2010 and several other e-mail programs refer to the address book entries as "contacts" and place them in a folder called Contacts. When you create a new contact, you enter the person's full name and e-mail address. You might also have the option to enter additional information about that person, including his or her personal and business mailing address, telephone number, cell phone number, Web page, instant message address, and even a picture.

* **Reduces errors and makes using e-mail quicker and more convenient**

  Being able to select a contact from your address book not only saves you time; it also reduces the chance that your message will not be delivered because you typed the e-mail address incorrectly. In most e-mail programs, if someone sends you a message, you can click the sender's address as well as other recipients' addresses in the top part of the message to add the addresses directly to your address book without any errors. Figure A-4 shows a sample address book from Outlook 2010.

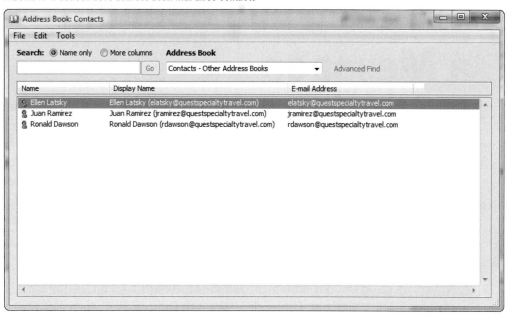

TABLE A-1: Examples of e-mail providers and addresses

e-mail sponsor	examples of service providers	description of e-mail services	where e-mail is stored	sample e-mail addresses
Corporate or company e-mail	Quest Specialty Travel	A company that provides e-mail for employees	Company server, or downloaded to user's computer	username@questspecialtytravel.com
Commercial provider: Cable TV, voice, and data communications companies	America Online, Comcast, Cablevision, EarthLink, Verizon	Also provide Web space and several e-mail addresses	ISP server, until downloaded to user's computer	username@aol.com username@comcast.net username@optimum.net username@earthlink.net username@verizon.net
Web-based e-mail	Hotmail (Microsoft), Gmail (Google), Yahoo! Mail (Yahoo!)	Web site that provides free e-mail addresses and service	On the Web site e-mail server	username@hotmail.com username@live.com username@gmail.com username@yahoo.com
Educational institution	Harvard University University of Delaware	Provide e-mail for faculty, staff, and students	On the university e-mail server	username@harvard.edu username@udel.edu

Creating and Sending a Message

When you create an e-mail message, you must indicate to whom you are sending the message and specify any people who should receive a copy. You also need to enter a meaningful subject for the message to give its recipients an idea of its content. You write the text of your message in the **message body**. After you create the message, you send it. Outlook 2010 uses Microsoft Word as the default text editor in e-mail messages, which means that you have access to the same text-formatting features in Outlook that you use when you create Word documents. Most e-mail programs use a basic text editor that enables you to do such things as change the color of text, use different fonts, create a bulleted list, and check the spelling of your message. You write and send a message to several employees about an upcoming meeting.

STEPS

1. **If you are using Outlook for e-mail, click the** Start button 🔘 **on the taskbar, click** All Programs, **click** Microsoft Office, **click** Microsoft Outlook 2010, **then click** Mail **if it is not already selected; if you are using Web-based e-mail, log into your e-mail account program**

   If you are using Outlook 2010 or another e-mail program, you can start the program and then create a message without connecting to the Internet. If your e-mail program is Web based, such as Hotmail or Gmail, you have to be connected to the Internet to create an e-mail message.

2. **Click the button or link that allows you to create new mail, such as the** New E-mail button **or the** Compose Mail button

   All e-mail programs provide a button or link to use to begin writing a new message. There are basic similarities in all programs, in that each new message window or page provides boxes or spaces to enter address information and message content, as shown in Figure A-5.

> **QUICK TIP**
> Use the e-mail address of a friend or associate to complete this lesson, or use your own e-mail address.

3. **Enter a valid e-mail address in the To text box as the address of the person to whom you are sending the message**

   You can send e-mail to more than one person at one time; just type each e-mail address in the To text box, and separate the addresses with a semicolon or comma (depending on what your e-mail program requires). You can also click the To button, or the Address Book button, to open the Select Names dialog box and select each e-mail address from the address book. If you click names or e-mail addresses in an address book, you are less likely to make an error as you enter addresses.

> **QUICK TIP**
> Bcc is available when you open the Select Names dialog box.

4. **Click the** Cc text box, **then type a friend's e-mail address as the e-mail address for a recipient who is to receive a courtesy copy**

   Cc stands for courtesy copy. **Courtesy copies** are typically sent to message recipients who need to be aware of the correspondence between the sender and the recipients. Bcc, or **blind courtesy copy**, is used when the sender does not want to reveal who he or she has sent courtesy copies to.

5. **Type** Meeting August 20 **in the Subject box as the subject for your message**

   The Subject text box should be a brief statement that indicates the purpose of your message. The subject becomes the title of the message.

> **QUICK TIP**
> Although you can write and read messages in Outlook and other programs when you are not online, you must be connected to the Internet to send or receive messages.

6. **Type your message in the message window**

   Figure A-6 shows a completed message. Many e-mail programs provide a spell-checking program that alerts you of spelling errors in your message. Messages should be concise and polite. If you want to send a lengthy message, consider attaching a file to the message. (You will learn about attaching files later in this unit.)

7. **Click the** Send button **to send your e-mail message**

   Once the message is sent, the message window or Web page closes. Most e-mail programs store a copy of the message in your Sent or Sent Items folder or give you the option to do so.

FIGURE A-5: New message window

Enter recipients' e-mail addresses here

Click the To button to open the Address book

Enter courtesy recipients' e-mail addresses here

Type message here

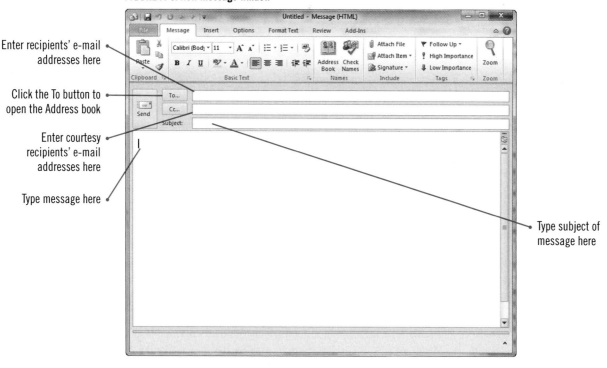

Type subject of message here

FIGURE A-6: A sample message

Send button

Subject message

Bulleted list in message body

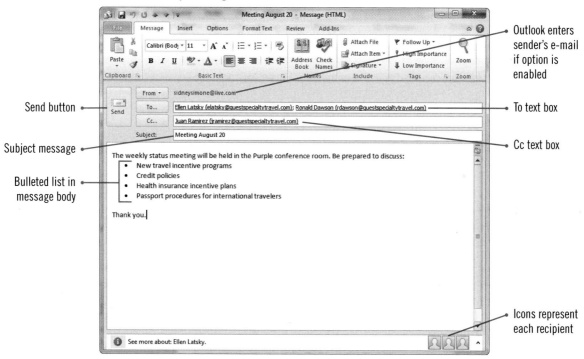

Outlook enters sender's e-mail if option is enabled

To text box

Cc text box

Icons represent each recipient

Understanding message headers

A **message header** contains the basic information about a message. It includes the sender's name and e-mail address, the names and e-mail addresses of recipients and Cc recipients, a date and time stamp, and the subject of the message. When e-mail travels through the e-mail system, the message header is the first information that you see when you retrieve your e-mail. Bcc recipients are not included in the message header. E-mail programs date- and time-stamp e-mail messages when they are received at the recipient's computer, using the current date and time.

Managing E-Mail Folders

Just as you save files in folders on your computer, you save e-mail messages in folders in your e-mail program. All e-mail programs provide a way for you to organize and save e-mail messages. You save messages so that you can refer to them again in the future. Most e-mail programs come with several default folders. These include Inbox, Drafts, Sent Items, Outbox, Deleted Items, and Junk E-mail folders (or folders with similar names). See Figure A-7. In addition, most allow you to create and name additional folders. Once you save messages, you can sort them within folders to help you find the message you want. As an employee of the Human Resources department, you send and receive messages on several topics. You organize the e-mail so you can better track the messages you send and receive.

DETAILS

E-mail programs come with the following default folders:

- **Inbox**

  An Inbox is a mail folder that receives all incoming e-mail as it arrives. You know who sent the e-mail message because the username or e-mail address and subject line appear in the list of e-mail in your Inbox, as shown in Figure A-8. You will also know when the message came in because your computer puts a date on it, which you can see along with the username and subject line. A closed envelope icon means the message has not been read yet. Many e-mail systems allow you to preview the message before opening a message. You can organize e-mail by date, sender, subject, and other header data.

- **Drafts**

  If you want to finish writing a message later, save it to store it in the Drafts folder. Many programs automatically save unsent messages at regular intervals in the drafts folder as a safety measure.

- **Sent Items**

  When you send a message, a copy of it is stored in the Sent Items folder. This folder helps you track the messages that you send out. You can change the settings on most e-mail programs so that you do not save messages to the Sent Items folder. You might not want to save all sent messages because they take up computer storage space.

- **Outbox**

  The Outbox is a temporary storage folder for messages that have not yet been sent. If you are working offline or if you set your e-mail program so that messages do not get sent immediately after you click the Send button, the messages are placed in the Outbox. When you connect to the Internet or click the Send/Receive All Folders button, the messages in the Outbox are sent.

- **Deleted Items or Trash**

  When you delete or erase a message from any folder, it is placed in the Deleted Items or Trash folder, rather than being immediately and permanently deleted. So if you delete a message accidentally, you can find it again. To empty the Deleted Items folder, right-click the folder or click a menu or toolbar button, and then click Empty Folder. Some programs have a special link to click in order to empty the folder. Some Web-based e-mail programs clear out the Trash folder if it gets too full or after messages have been in the folder for a specified period of time.

QUICK TIP

You should clear out the Sent Items and Deleted Items folders periodically to free up storage space on your computer.

- **Junk E-Mail or Spam**

  Junk e-mail, or **spam**, is unwanted e-mail that arrives from unsolicited sources. Most junk e-mail is advertising or offensive messages. **Spamming** is the sending of identical or near-identical unsolicited messages to a large number of recipients. Many e-mail programs have filters that identify this type of e-mail and place it in a special folder. Then you can easily delete the e-mail you don't want. It is possible that a message that you do want might get caught by the spam filter. It is good practice to look at the headers in the Junk E-mail folder before deleting the messages stored there.

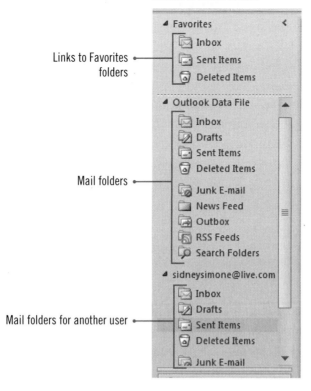

Links to Favorites folders

Mail folders

Mail folders for another user

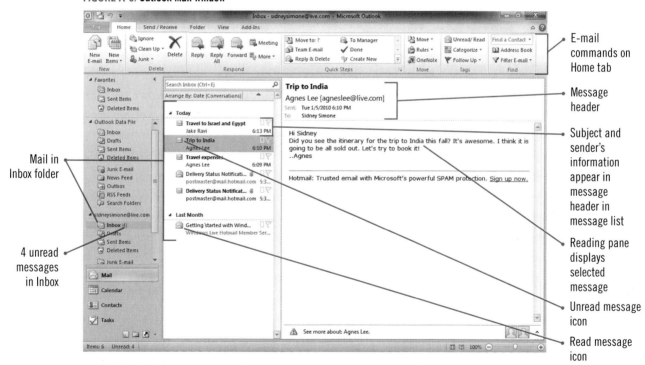

Mail in Inbox folder

4 unread messages in Inbox

E-mail commands on Home tab

Message header

Subject and sender's information appear in message header in message list

Reading pane displays selected message

Unread message icon

Read message icon

Sorting your mail

You would be surprised at how quickly your Inbox, Sent Items, and Deleted Items or Trash folders can fill up. How can you manage these? The best way is to create folders for specific projects or people that you know will be "high volume" for e-mail. For example, if you are working on a special project, create a folder for that project. Any e-mail that you receive or send about the project can be moved into that folder. Depending on your e-mail program, you can also categorize, flag, or label messages. You can sort e-mail by any message header, such as date, subject, flag or label, or sender to find an important message quickly. Once the project is completed, you can archive or delete that folder's e-mail. Check to see how much e-mail is accumulating in the Deleted Items or Trash folder. E-mail takes up storage space, and if you are running out of storage on your computer, your e-mail is a good place to start cleaning up the hard drive.

Receiving and Replying to a Message

To read a message that arrives in your Inbox, you first select it. Outlook and some other e-mail software programs let you preview a selected message in the Reading or Preview Pane. To open the message in its own window, you can double-click the message header. After reading a message, you can delete it, move it to another folder, flag it for follow-up, or keep it in your Inbox. You can also send a response back to the sender of the message by clicking the Reply button. You often reply to messages sent to you as you correspond with the staff at QST.

STEPS

1. **Open a new message window, enter** your e-mail address **in the To text box, type** Learning how to use e-mail **as the subject, then for the body of the message, type** I am sending this message to myself to learn how to send and reply to messages.

> **TROUBLE**
> You might have to check for mail several times before the e-mail message comes in.

2. **Click the** Send button **in the message window, click the** Send/Receive tab, **click the** Send/Receive All Folders button **in the Send & Receive group, then open the** Inbox **in the e-mail program**

   When you click the Send/Receive or Get Mail button, your e-mail program checks for any messages in the Outbox that need to be sent and delivers incoming messages to your Inbox. Many e-mail programs deliver e-mail to the Inbox at the time you sign in or log in with your username and password.

> **QUICK TIP**
> In many Web-based e-mail programs, you have to click the Get Mail button or link, and clicking an e-mail message opens the message.

3. **Click the** Learning how to use e-mail message **in the Inbox to select it and view the message**

   You can read the message header to identify the message by subject, date, and sender. If your e-mail has a preview feature, you can preview the message before you open it by clicking its header. In Outlook, the message appears in the Reading Pane in the Outlook window. You might have to click a link or button to display inserted graphics or video. Many programs hide images to protect your privacy, unless you configure the program's settings to accept images for each message in the Inbox.

4. **Double-click the** Learning how to use e-mail message **in the inbox to open it in a new window, read the message, then click the message window's** Close button ✕

5. **Right-click the** Learning how to use e-mail message header, **then point to** Quick Steps

   Figure A-9 shows the Outlook shortcut menu and Quick Steps submenu. Reply lets you reply to the original sender. The Reply All option lets you reply to the original sender and all the Cc recipients of the original message. Bcc recipients are not included in Reply or Reply All messages. The Quick Steps submenu offers a list of customizable command sequences that also appear in the Quick Steps group on the Home tab. For example, Reply & Delete both replies to the message and deletes the original to help keep your Inbox clean.

> **QUICK TIP**
> Depending on how you set up your e-mail program, you can automatically include or exclude the text of the original sender's message in the message body along with the message header.

6. **Click the** message **to close the menus, click the** Home tab, **then click the** Reply button **in the Respond group**

   Clicking the Reply button automatically opened a new message window addressed to the original sender. The subject line is preceded by "RE:", indicating that the message is a reply. The header from the original message appears above the original message. The insertion point is at the top of the message body. See Figure A-10.

7. **Type** This is my reply message. **in the message body as the reply**

   It is helpful to include the original message in a reply to help the message recipient recall the topic.

8. **Click the** Send button **in the message window**

   The message is sent, and a copy of it is stored in your Sent Items folder. Most e-mail programs add a Replied to Message icon next to the original message in the Inbox, indicating that you have replied to the message. Often this is a small arrow pointing to the left.

9. **Close the original message if necessary to return to the Inbox**

FIGURE A-9: Message options

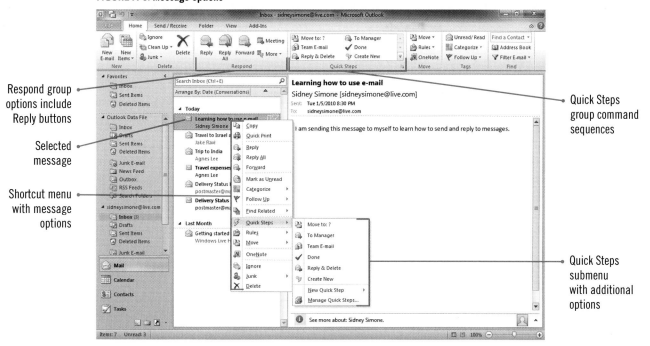

Respond group options include Reply buttons

Selected message

Shortcut menu with message options

Quick Steps group command sequences

Quick Steps submenu with additional options

FIGURE A-10: Replying to a message

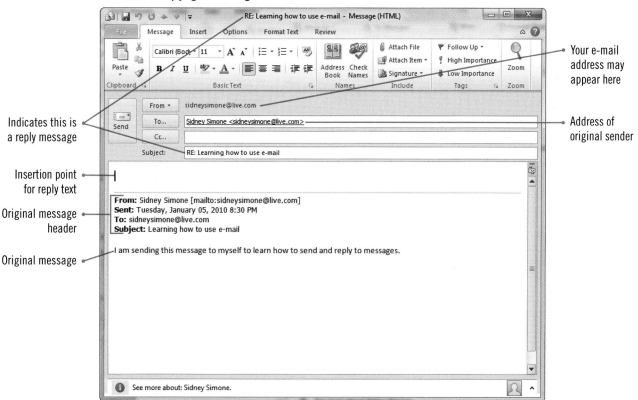

Indicates this is a reply message

Insertion point for reply text

Original message header

Original message

Your e-mail address may appear here

Address of original sender

Setting up vacation responses

Most e-mail programs allow you to set up an automatic response or vacation message if you are not going to be able to get your e-mail for a specified period of time. This is a helpful way to let people know that you are not ignoring any e-mail they send, but rather that you are not reading your e-mail. When vacation mode is active, your e-mail program automatically sends out a reply when a message comes in. You determine the content of the reply message. A typical message might be "Thank you for your message. I am on vacation from July 1–July 10th and will respond to your message when I return." Most e-mail programs only send one automatic response to each sender each day or within a specified period of time.

Forwarding a Message

You might receive e-mail that you need to send to someone else. Sending a message you have received from one person to someone else is called **forwarding**. When you forward a message, you send it to people who have not already received it—that is, people not in the To or Cc text boxes of the original message. You can include an additional message about the forwarded message in the message body. The subject of the forwarded message stays the same, so you can organize it by subject with any other messages on the same topic, with the same subject heading. In most e-mail programs, you forward a message that you have received to another person by clicking the Forward button. At QST, you sometimes get e-mail from clients that you forward to the travel agents at their branch offices for their information.

STEPS

1. **Click the Send/Receive tab, then click the Send/Receive All Folders button or click the Get Mail or Check Mail button or link in your e-mail program**

   Your e-mail program checks for any messages in the Outbox that need to be sent and delivers any incoming messages to your Inbox.

2. **Select a message that you want to forward, if it is not selected, then click the message in the Inbox**

   You read the message header to identify the message. You can see the original recipients of the message by reviewing the header. You can see who, if anyone, got the message by reviewing the e-mail addresses in the To and Cc areas of the header. You will not know who might have received a Bcc on the message. When you view a message, you see buttons for several options available to you after you read it. One of the options is to click the Forward button to forward the message.

   QUICK TIP
   To display the From e-mail address in a message window, click the Options tab, in the Show Fields group, then click From.

3. **Click the Home tab on the Ribbon, then click the Forward button in the Respond group**

   A New Message window opens, containing the original message. Clicking the Forward button does not automatically address the e-mail to anyone; all address fields are blank. The original message is included in the body of the message. The subject line is preceded by "FW:", indicating that the message is a forwarded one. Most e-mail software includes the message header from the original message in the Message window above the original message. The insertion point is at the top of the message window in the To field. You can address this message as you would any new e-mail. You can include multiple recipients, including Cc and Bcc recipients. If you want to provide a courtesy note explaining the forward, you can click in the message body above the original message header and type a brief note.

4. **Type a friend's e-mail address in the To text box, then type I thought you might like to read this message. in the message body above the forwarded message, as shown in Figure A-11**

5. **Click the Send button in the message window**

   The message is sent, and a copy of it is stored in your Sent Items folder. Most e-mail programs add a Forwarded Message icon next to the original message, indicating that you have forwarded the message. Often this is a small arrow pointing to the right.

6. **Close the original message if necessary to return to the Inbox**

FIGURE A-11: Forwarding a message

Indicates this is a forwarded message

New text for message

Forwarded message

Friend's e-mail address

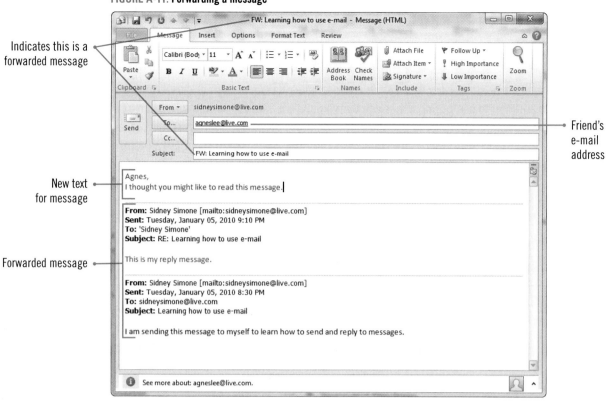

Flagging or labeling messages

Most e-mail programs provide a way to identify or categorize e-mail. If you use e-mail for business, school, or personal communication, you will find that you receive many e-mail messages. Some can be read and discarded. Others require additional attention or follow-up. Organizing your e-mail can help you keep up with the many messages you are likely to receive. If you are using Outlook, flags can assist you in your effort to manage your e-mail. If you click the flag icon next to the message, it is marked by default with a red Quick Flag. However, you can use flags of different shades of red to mark messages for different categories of follow-up. In Outlook, flags are available for Today, Tomorrow, This Week, Next Week, No Date, and Custom; the Today flag is the darkest shade of red, and the This Week and Next Week flags are the lightest. To apply a flag, click the flag in the message you want to flag. To select from a list of flag actions and specify a due date in the Custom dialog box, right-click a message, point to Follow Up, then click Add Reminder. Outlook also allows you to color code messages for categories. See Figure A-12. If you are using Web-based e-mail, you might have other options for categorizing, labelling, or flagging e-mail. For example, Gmail provides a way to assign a label to e-mail or to star e-mail for easy sorting or organizing.

FIGURE A-12: Flagging and categorizing messages

Flag

Categories

Sending a Message with an Attachment

In addition to composing a message by typing in the Message window, you can **attach** a file to an e-mail message. For example, in an office environment, employees can attach Word or Excel documents to e-mail messages so that other employees can open them, make changes to them, and then return them to the original sender or forward them to others for review. You can attach any type of computer file to an e-mail message, including pictures, video, and audio. Keep in mind that to open an attachment created using a particular software program, the recipient of the attachment might need to have the appropriate software. You often send clients' trip photos to people in the office. You also have to send personnel documents to employees throughout the year. Attaching files is a common task in your job in the Human Resources department.

STEPS

QUICK TIP

Many e-mail programs will complete a previously used address once you start typing in the To box. You can click the address or press [Tab] to select the address to enter it into the To text box.

1. **Click the New E-mail button in the New group or click the button or link to open a new mail message window, then type your e-mail address in the To text box**

   You can send a message with an attachment to more than one person at one time; just enter each e-mail address in the To text box, separated by a semicolon or comma, just as you would an e-mail without an attachment. You can also click the Cc text box or Bcc text box, and then enter e-mail addresses for recipients who are to receive a Cc or Bcc.

2. **Type LNT Talking Points in the Subject box as the subject for the message, then in the message window, type Please review these Leave No Trace talking points for the National Parks presentation.**

3. **If you are using Outlook, click the Attach File button in the Include group on the Message tab**

   Most e-mail programs provide a way to attach files, either with an Attach link or with an Attach a File or Attach button. The name of the command or way to access the dialog box might differ slightly. Once the Insert File or Attach File dialog box opens, files appear in a dialog box as shown in Figures A-13 and A-14. You might have to click a Browse button to navigate to the file or files you want to attach. Often you can use the Thumbnails view in the dialog box to see what the files look like before you attach them to a message.

4. **Navigate to the drive and folder where you store your Data Files, click Leave No Trace.docx, then click Insert, Open, or Attach**

   Most programs will allow you to attach more than one file to a message. Some Internet service providers will limit message size or the number of attachments for one e-mail. Attachments such as movies might be too large for some e-mail systems to handle. Once attached, files appear in the Attached text box or another area of the message window. Often, an icon next to each filename indicates the type of file it is. The numbers in parentheses next to the filenames specify the size of each file. As a general rule, try to keep the total size of attachments below 1 MB. Also, consider the Internet connection speed of the recipient's computer. If a recipient does not have a fast Internet connection, a large file could take a long time to download.

5. **Send the message**

FIGURE A-13: Attaching a file in Outlook

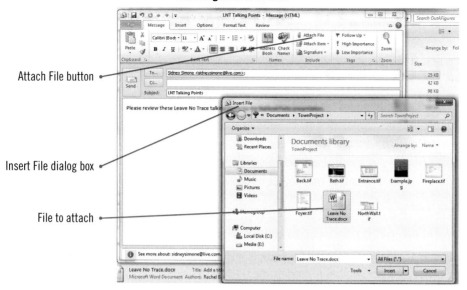

Attach File button

Insert File dialog box

File to attach

FIGURE A-14: Attaching a file using Hotmail

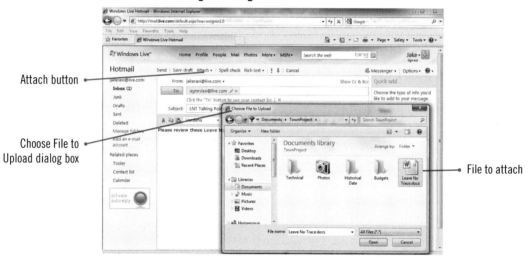

Attach button

Choose File to Upload dialog box

File to attach

Reviewing options when sending messages

E-mail programs can have several options that affect how messages are delivered. To change these options in Outlook, click the Options tab in the Message window to view the Message Options, then click the launcher in the More Options group to open the Properties dialog box shown in Figure A-15. You can, for example, assign a level of importance and a level of sensitivity so that the reader can prioritize messages. You can also encrypt the message for privacy. If both the sender and recipient are using Outlook, you can add Voting buttons to your message for recipients to use in responding. In addition, when you want to know when a message has been received or read, you can select the Request a delivery receipt for this message check box or the Request a read receipt for this message check box. You can also specify a future date for delivering a message if the timing of the message is important. Lastly, if you want replies to your message to be sent to a different e-mail address than your own, you can click the "Have replies sent to" check box and then specify a new destination address for replies.

FIGURE A-15: Message options

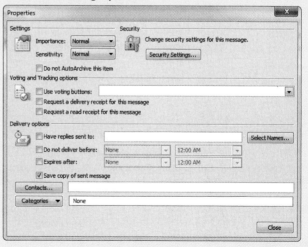

Employing Good E-Mail Practices

E-mail has become the standard for business correspondence. It has also become an accepted standard for personal communication as well as communication between students and teachers. Although it is an easy and fast way to communicate, there are many considerations to keep in mind before sending e-mail. Working in the Human Resources department, you are responsible for corporate policy relating to e-mail. You send out a memo that outlines the company policy for e-mail.

DETAILS

The following are good practices to follow when sending and receiving e-mail:

- **Be considerate:** Always be polite and use proper spelling and grammar in e-mail messages. Be sure to use the spelling checker as a last step before sending messages.

> **QUICK TIP**
> Consider using compression software to reduce the size of any attachment that exceeds the limit but must be sent.

- **Consider file size:** Unless you have consulted with the recipient and know that he or she can receive large file attachments, avoid sending any attachment that exceeds 1 MB.

- **Be safe:** Never open an e-mail message unless you know who sent it to you. Keep your spam filter, spyware software, and virus software up to date. Be sure to run the virus checker through all received e-mail. Keeping computers safe from viruses and spyware is very important.

- **Think before forwarding:** Before you forward a message, consider the contents of the message and the privacy of the person who sent the message. A joke, a story, or anything that is not personal usually can be forwarded without invading the sender's privacy. When you are certain the sender would not mind having his or her message forwarded, you can forward the message to others.

- **Be professional:** In very casual correspondence, you can present an informal message by using shortcuts like "LOL" for "laughing out loud" and "BRB!" for "be right back!" However, limit this technique to personal messages. Any e-mail that is intended for professional use or is a reflection on a professional organization should not use shortcuts.

> **QUICK TIP**
> The use of emoticons should also be limited to informal e-mail among close colleagues or friends, not professional correspondence.

- **Limit emoticons:** You can use emoticons in your text to show how you are feeling. You create an emoticon by combining more than one keyboard character to make a graphic. For example, type a colon and a closing parenthesis to make a smiley face ☺.

- **Maintain your account:** Outlook offers cleanup tools, as shown in Figure A-16. Most programs offer similar tools for maintaining your folders. When you are finished using an e-mail program, it is good practice to delete or archive e-mail messages that you no longer need. If working for a company, you should comply with corporate policy. For personal e-mail, you should periodically delete unneeded messages from the Sent Items folder to help manage storage on your computer. It is also good practice to empty the Trash folder. To delete a message, select it, then click the Delete button in the Delete group on the Home tab, or press [Delete]. To empty the Trash or Deleted Items folder, right-click the folder, then click Empty Folder, Empty Trash, or Empty Deleted Items folder. When you see a confirmation message, as shown in Figure A-17, click Yes.

Controlling your message

When you communicate with e-mail, take extra care in what you say and how you say it. The recipient of an e-mail message cannot see body language or hear the tone of voice to interpret the meaning of the message. For example, using all capital letters in the text of a message is the e-mail equivalent of shouting and is not appropriate. Carefully consider the content of a message before you send it, and don't send confidential or sensitive material. Remember, once you send a message, you might not be able to prevent it from being delivered. E-mail is not private; you cannot control who might read the message once it has been sent. Do not write anything in an e-mail that you would not write on a postcard that you send through the postal service. If your e-mail account is a company account, be sure you know the policy on whether or not your company permits the sending of personal messages. All messages you send through an employer's e-mail system legally belong to the company for which you work, so don't assume that your messages are private.

FIGURE A-16: Cleanup tools

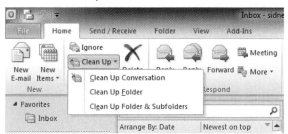

FIGURE A-17: Deleting items

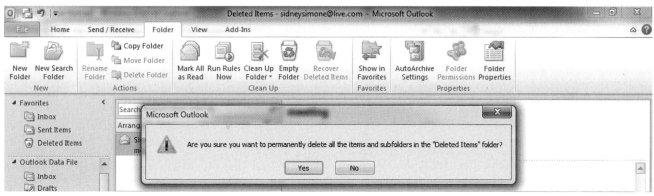

Creating distribution lists

When using an e-mail program to communicate with friends or coworkers, you might find that you need to send messages to the same group of people on a regular basis. If your address book contains many contacts, it can take time to scroll through all the names to select the ones you want, and you might forget to include someone in an important message. Fortunately, e-mail programs provide an easy way to group your contacts. You can create a **distribution list**, or a **contact group**, which is a collection of contacts to whom you want to send the same messages. Distribution lists, or contact groups, make it possible for you to send a message to the same group of e-mail addresses without having to select each contact in the group. For example, if you send messages reminding your Human Resources staff of a weekly meeting, you can create a distribution list called "HR-STAFF" that contains the names and e-mail addresses of your staff who must attend the meeting. When you want to send a message to everyone on the team, you simply select HR-STAFF from the address book, instead of selecting each person's name individually. Once you create a distribution list, you can add new members to it or delete members from it as necessary. If you change information about a contact that is part of a group or list, the list is automatically updated.

Practice

For current SAM information, including versions and content details, visit SAM Central (http://www.cengage.com/samcentral). If you have a SAM user profile, you may have access to hands-on instruction, practice, and assessment of the skills covered in this unit. Since various versions of SAM are supported throughout the life of this text, check with your instructor for the correct instructions and URL/Web site for accessing assignments.

Concepts Review

Label each element of the New Message window shown in Figure A-18.

FIGURE A-18

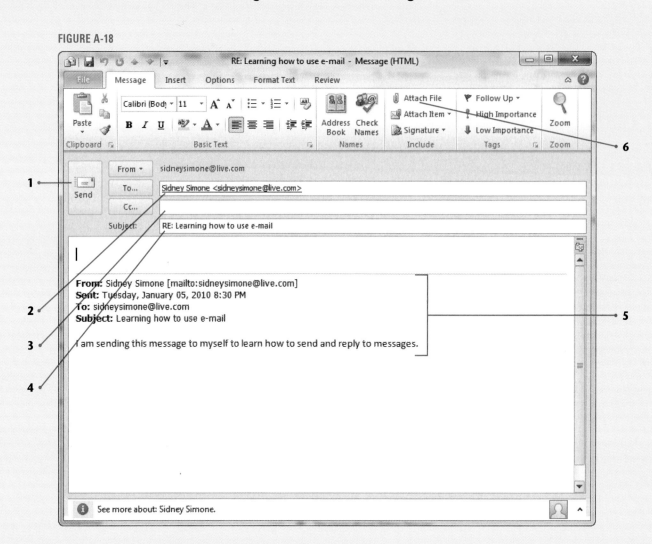

Match each term with the statement that best describes it.

7. sidneysimone@live.com
8. FW
9. Bcc
10. Sent Items folder
11. Inbox
12. Address book

a. Stores names and e-mail addresses
b. An e-mail address
c. Stores all e-mail that you send out
d. Identifies a forwarded message
e. Contains messages you have received
f. Hides e-mail address of recipient to all others

Select the best answer from the list of choices.

13. Any e-mail received as part of large unsolicited mailing is best placed automatically in the _____.
    - **a.** Junk E-Mail or Spam folder
    - **b.** Deleted Items folder
    - **c.** Sent Items folder
    - **d.** Inbox

14. If you do not want the recipients of your message to see the others who got the same message, you should use the _____ feature.
    - **a.** Cc
    - **b.** Bcc
    - **c.** Outbox
    - **d.** flag

15. Your e-mail _____ can be files of any type, such as documents, spreadsheets, video, images, and sound files.
    - **a.** attachments
    - **b.** headers
    - **c.** drafts
    - **d.** first three lines of the message body

16. If you want people who send you an e-mail message to get a message from you even if you can't view or respond to their message right away, you should set up a(n) _____.
    - **a.** voting and tracking option
    - **b.** vacation response
    - **c.** delivery option
    - **d.** importance setting

17. E-mail that you have finished writing but has not yet been sent is stored in the _____.
    - **a.** Inbox
    - **b.** New Mail folder
    - **c.** Outbox
    - **d.** Sent Items folder

18. When you forward a selected message to another person, the e-mail addresses for the original recipients of the message _____.
    - **a.** appear only in the To text box
    - **b.** do not appear in any text box
    - **c.** appear only in the Cc text box
    - **d.** appear in the To and the Cc text boxes

19. The _____ feature helps you follow up and organize messages.
    - **a.** folders
    - **b.** flag
    - **c.** Bcc
    - **d.** FW

20. To ensure that you send the same message to the same group of multiple recipients, set up a(n) _____.
    - **a.** address book
    - **b.** Quick Step
    - **c.** Draft folder
    - **d.** contact group or distribution list

Skills Review

1. **Start Outlook or your e-mail program and view the Inbox.**
    - **a.** Start Outlook or your e-mail program.
    - **b.** If necessary, select the mail part of the program.
    - **c.** Click the Send/Receive All Folders button or link to get new e-mail delivered to the Inbox, if necessary.
    - **d.** Open the Inbox to view any new messages.

2. **Create and send a message.**
    - **a.** Open a new message window.
    - **b.** Click the To text box, then type a friend's e-mail address.
    - **c.** Type your e-mail address in the Cc text box.
    - **d.** Type **Employee Discount Travel Program** as the subject of the message.
    - **e.** In the message body, type **Please be sure to process your travel invoices with the correct codes to get your discount.**
    - **f.** Send the message.

Skills Review (continued)

3. Manage e-mail folders.

   a. Review the mail folders in your e-mail program.

   b. Look for a Sent Items or Sent folder and see if the Employee Discount Travel Program message is in that folder.

   c. Open the Deleted Items or Trash folder. See if any e-mail is in that folder.

   d. Review the Spam or Junk E-Mail folder.

4. Receive and reply to a message.

   a. If necessary, click the Send/Receive All Folders button to deliver messages to your Inbox.

   b. Display the contents of the Inbox folder.

   c. Read the message from yourself.

   d. Click the Reply button.

   e. In the message body, type **Is there a list of codes in the handbook?**, then send the message.

5. Forward a message.

   a. Forward the message you received to another friend.

   b. In the top of the forwarded message body, type **This important message came to me from HR, be sure to read the entire message.** (Refer to Figure A-19.)

   c. Send the message.

   d. Close the original message.

FIGURE A-19

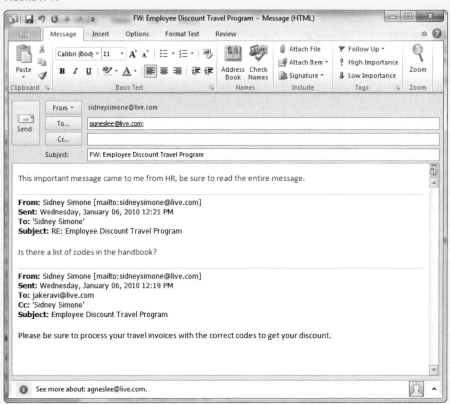

6. Send a message with an attachment.

   a. Create a new e-mail message.

   b. Enter your e-mail address as the message recipient.

   c. Enter a friend's e-mail address in the Cc text box.

   d. Enter **Travel photo** as the subject of the message.

   e. In the message body, type **Here is the photo from my trip to New York.**

   f. Click the Insert File, Attach File, or Attach button or link.

   g. Navigate to the drive and folder where you store your Data Files.

Skills Review (continued)

h. Select the file Bridge.jpg (see Figure A-20), then click Insert, Open, or Attach (depending on your program).

i. Send the message.

FIGURE A-20

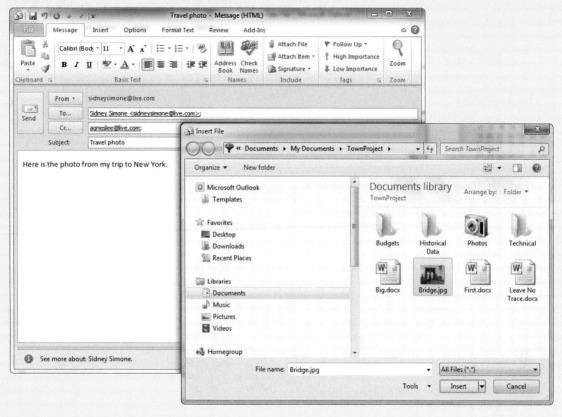

7. Delete items.

a. Delete all of the messages received in this exercise from the Inbox folder.

b. Delete all of the messages sent in this exercise from the Sent Items folder.

c. Empty the Deleted Items folder.

d. Exit the e-mail program.

Independent Challenge 1

You are a member of the zoning and development board in your town. You have been appointed to chair the committee to investigate a proposal for developing a two-acre section of town under the Green Acres Project. You decide to use e-mail to communicate with the other members of the committee as well as with the local newspaper, the town council, and the mayor.

a. Start Outlook or your e-mail program.

b. Open the address book and add yourself as well as three other new contacts to the address book. Use the names and e-mail addresses of classmates, teachers, or friends. (*Hint*: In Outlook, the Address Book button is in the Find group on the Home tab of the Mail window.)

c. Create a new message and address it to yourself, then use the Cc field to send this message to two of the new contacts.

d. Type **Green Acres Project** as the subject of the message.

e. In the message body, type **There will be a public hearing on Thursday at 8:00 p.m. We should prepare our presentation and contact the local newspaper to be sure they carry the story.**

Independent Challenge 1 (continued)

f. Press [Enter], then type your name. See Figure A-21.

g. Send the message, then click the Send/Receive All Folders button if necessary. Depending on the speed and type of Internet connection you are using, you might need to click the Send/Receive button again, after waiting a few moments, if you do not receive the e-mail in your Inbox the first time you click the Send/Receive button.

h. Open the message in the Inbox, flag it with a follow-up flag or other symbol, then print it.

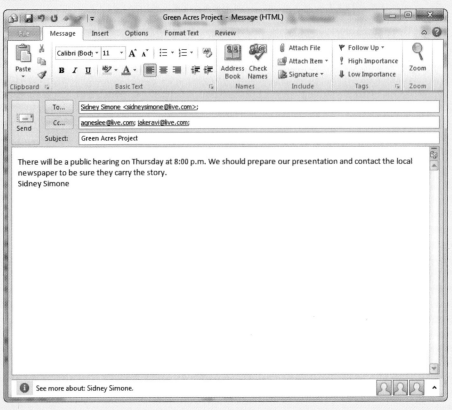

Advanced Challenge Exercise

- Forward the message to the person you did not include in the distribution list.
- In the message body, type **Forgot to include you in this mailing! Please read the message; hope you can be there.**
- Send the message.

i. Delete all of the messages related to this Independent Challenge from the Inbox folder.

j. Delete all of the messages related to this Independent Challenge from the Sent Items folder.

k. Delete the contacts that you added in this Independent Challenge from the address book.

l. Empty the Deleted Items folder.

m. Exit the e-mail program.

Independent Challenge 2

You are planning a study trip to India with a group from the university. You have to send e-mail messages with an attachment as you organize this trip.

a. Start Outlook or your e-mail program, then create a new message and address it to two contacts, such as friends, family members, or classmates.

b. Enter your e-mail address in the Cc text box.

c. Type **Trip to Mumbai** in the Subject text box.

d. Start your word processor and write a brief letter to your friends to encourage them to join you on the adventure. Conclude the document with a personal note about why you want to participate in a study program. Save the document file in the drive and folder where you store your Data Files, using a filename you will remember.

e. Type a short note in the message body of the e-mail to the recipients of the message, telling them that you thought they would like to join you on this trip and that you are looking forward to them joining you.

f. Attach the word-processing document to the message.

g. Send the message, then click the Send/Receive All Folders button. Depending on the speed and type of Internet connection you are using, you might need to click the Send/Receive button again, after waiting a few moments, if you do not receive a response e-mail the first time you click the Send/Receive button.

h. Print a copy of the message you receive in response.

Advanced Challenge Exercise

- Locate a picture or graphic image file on your computer that you want to send through e-mail.
- Right-click the picture, point to Send to, then click Mail recipient on the shortcut menu. (Alternatively, after right-clicking a picture, you might see these options: E-mail Picture or E-mail with [e-mail program]. These options will be different depending on your software and system.) Click OK if a dialog box opens asking if you want to make the picture smaller. Click Attach to attach the image to a new message window.
- When a new message window opens, enter your e-mail address in the To text box, then write a brief message in the body of the message. Add Bcc and Cc recipients. Set a priority level. Use Figure A-22 as a guide.
- Send the message, then read the message and view the picture when it arrives in your Inbox.

FIGURE A-22

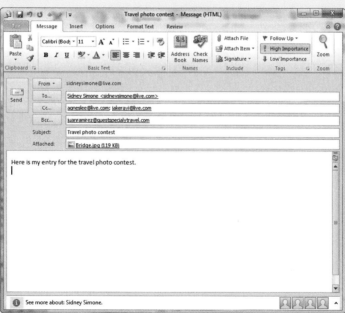

i. Delete all of the messages received for this Independent Challenge from your Inbox.

j. Delete all of the messages sent for this Independent Challenge from the Sent Items folder.

k. Empty the Deleted Items folder.

l. Exit Outlook.

Visual Workshop

Refer to the e-mail message in Figure A-23 to complete this Visual Workshop. Use your e-mail program to create and then send this message. Be sure to send the message to at least one recipient. Attach a file that you created on your computer. It can be a document, worksheet, image, or database file.

FIGURE A-23

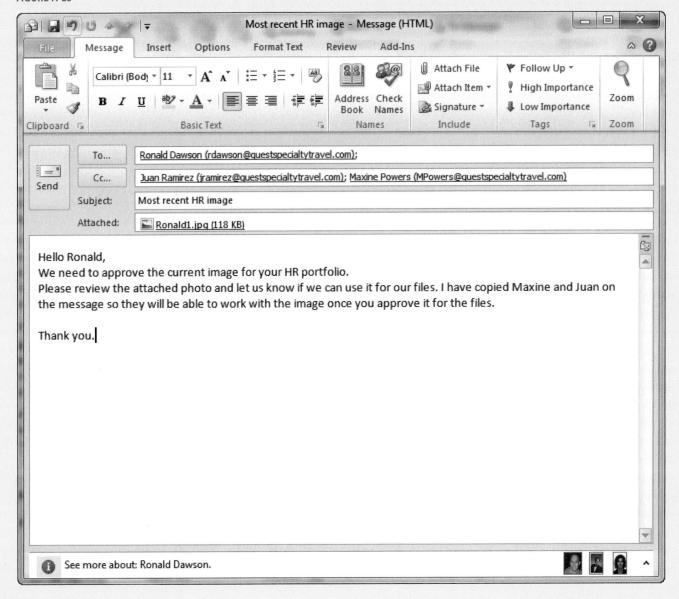

Getting Started with E-Mail

Managing Information Using Outlook

Files You Will Need:

No files needed.

While Outlook lets you easily manage your e-mail, it can do a lot more. Outlook is a complete personal information and time management program you can use for all your business and personal information. Outlook integrates E-mail, Calendar, Contacts, Tasks, Notes, and Journal modules that let you manage your mail, appointments and activities, address book, to-do list, and notes all in one program. ▬▬ Now that you know how to send, receive, and manage your e-mail, you will learn how to use Outlook as a desktop information manager to help you organize your schedule, to-do list, communications, and associates.

OBJECTIVES

Start Outlook

Organize e-mail

Add contacts

Manage appointments

Manage tasks

Create notes

Use the Journal

Apply categories

Starting Outlook

The Outlook screen is fully customizable to let you view your contacts, schedule, or mail with different levels of detail. You can change how the data is organized and sorted. The first time you start Outlook, you will be prompted to set up a personal **account** that identifies you as a user. If you want to use Outlook for e-mail, you must enter your e-mail address and password, the type of Internet service provider (ISP) you are using, and the incoming and outgoing mail server address for your ISP. You can set up more than one account in a single installation of Outlook. Each user has a username and password for his or her account. ▰▰▰▰ As the assistant to Juan Ramirez in the Human Resources department, you learn Outlook so you can use it for communication and scheduling. Refer to Figure B-1, which shows the Outlook Mail window, as you read about how to customize the window.

STEPS

TROUBLE
Because Outlook is fully customizable and depends on the accounts that have been set up, your screen will look different than the figures in this book. You might also see some differences in the menus.

1. **Click the** Start button **on the taskbar** ⊙**, point to** All Programs**, click** Microsoft Office**, then click** Microsoft Outlook 2010 **to start Outlook**

   Figure B-1 shows a typical Outlook window when you select Mail. The **Navigation Pane** lets you choose a module as well as specific areas within that module. In Figure B-1, the lower portion of the Navigation Pane shows that Mail is selected. You can click the Calendar, Contacts, or Tasks buttons to work with those Outlook modules. When Mail is selected, the upper part of the Navigation Pane shows the Folder List. The Inbox folder is where you get your new e-mail messages. The Reading Pane lets you read the selected e-mail message. The To-Do Bar includes the Date Navigator, appointments for the current week, and your upcoming tasks. The **People Pane** shows you any social media information available for the person sending the current message and included files, appointments, and notes related to that person.

2. **Click the** View tab **on the Ribbon, click the** Navigation Pane button **in the Layout group, click** Normal**, click the** Reading Pane button**, then click** Right

   The options on the View tab let you determine how the Navigation Pane, To-Do Bar, and Reading Pane appear in each of the Outlook modules. When you select Normal, the Navigation Pane appears on the left side of the screen. When you select Minimized, the Navigation Pane appears as a vertical bar along the left side of the Outlook window and shows only the module navigation and folder buttons.

   QUICK TIP
   If a To-Do Bar item does not have a check mark, click it once to select it.

3. **On the View tab, click the** To-Do Bar **button in the Layout group, then verify that there are check marks next to** Normal, Date Navigator, Appointments, **and** Task List

   The To-Do Bar, which appears on the right side of the window in Figure B-1, shows you what you need to do for the day. A calendar called the **Date Navigator** gives you an overview of the month. You can minimize the To-Do Bar so that it appears as a vertical bar on the right side of the window by clicking the Minimize the To-Do Bar button. You can also open the To-Do Bar Options dialog box, shown in Figure B-2, and adjust To-Do Bar display options. To open the To-Do Bar Options dialog box, click the To-Do Bar button in the Layout group, then click Options.

4. **Click the** Home tab **on the Ribbon, click the** More button ⊡ **in the Quick Steps group, then click** Manage Quick Steps

   The Manage Quick Steps dialog box opens. See Figure B-3. Quick Steps are shortcuts that help you complete basic Outlook tasks with one click. You can set up Quick Steps for your own tasks or create your own Quick Steps based on other common e-mail tasks.

   QUICK TIP
   Drag the border between the Folder List and module buttons in the Navigation Pane to expand or shrink the list and minimize or maximize the buttons.

5. **Click** Cancel **to close the Manage Quick Steps dialog box**

6. **In the Navigation Pane, click** Calendar**, click** Contacts**, click** Tasks**, click the** Notes button ▱**, click the** Folder List button ▱**, then review the screen content after each view change**

   Mail, Calendar, Contacts, Tasks, Notes, and Journal are the modules in Outlook. The Journal module does not appear by default in the Outlook window. You will learn more about the Journal later in this unit. The Folder List shows you the available folders for storing your e-mail, calendar, contacts, and journal entries. You can open any of these modules by clicking the Navigation Pane. The Folder List in the Navigation Pane displays each folder under Personal Folders with Outlook items specific to your account.

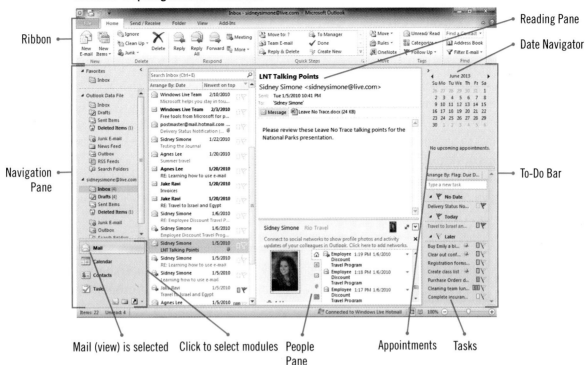

FIGURE B-1: Opening screen in Outlook Mail

Ribbon

Navigation Pane

Mail (view) is selected   Click to select modules   People Pane

Reading Pane

Date Navigator

To-Do Bar

Appointments   Tasks

FIGURE B-2: To-Do Bar Options dialog box

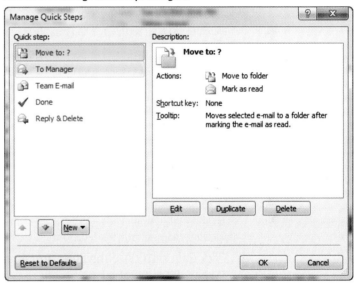

FIGURE B-3: Manage Quick Steps dialog box

Explaining RSS

The Internet has many Web sites that provide an overwhelming amount and variety of information. News sites are updated hourly; some corporations deliver news about products daily; there are entertainment Web sites that provide information about films and shows weekly; and many organizations keep their sites current. To stay on top of all this changing information, you would have to visit each site each day—a seemingly impossible task. Fortunately, there are technologies on the Internet that can help you stay current in topics that interest you. **Really Simple Syndication (RSS)** is a format for "feeding" or "syndicating" news or any content from Web sites to your computer. Outlook provides a way to have this information

come directly into an RSS Feeds folder. Click the Folder List button in the Navigation Pane to see the RSS Feeds folder. Access to RSS content is free, but you have to subscribe to a Web site that offers RSS feeds. RSS feeds provide subscribers with summaries that link to the full versions of the content. Once you see that you want to read more about the topic, you can click the link to view the article in the Reading Pane. You can organize the RSS feeds by creating folders for each topic or Web site that you subscribe to. The advantage to using RSS is that you may select different types of information from a variety of Web sites and view them all at the same time.

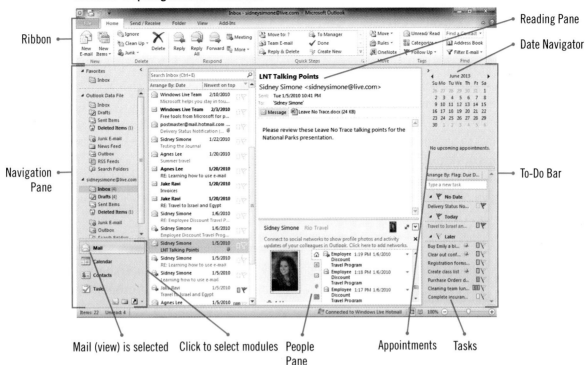

Organizing E-Mail

You can create and send e-mail using any e-mail program; most essential features are the same across the programs. If you use Outlook Mail as your e-mail program, you can use it to organize your e-mail, such as by conversation, view, or folder. Use the Contact module to store your e-mail addresses and get meeting requests through e-mail that then become appointments on your Calendar. You can search messages for specific content, dates, or senders. All new e-mail arrives in the Inbox folder unless you set up rules to deliver e-mail in other folders. A **rule** is an action you can create to have Outlook automatically handle particular messages in a certain way. By default, Outlook displays e-mail in Conversation view and **sorts**, or orders, the e-mail by date. To specify a different view, click the View tab, then select from the options in the Arrangement group.   You will receive e-mail from clients and QST employees. You set up Outlook to view and manage the e-mail using its many organizational features.

1. **Click Mail in the Navigation Pane, click the Inbox in the Mail Folders list, click the View tab on the Ribbon, click the To-Do Bar button in the Layout group, then click Off**

   Outlook Mail is now the active module, and the To-Do Bar is closed. See Figure B-4. You see a list of all Mail folders in the Navigation Pane, divided into sections. The Favorites section contains shortcuts to folders that you use most often. The folders are divided by user account. Each user account has a Mail Folders section with all available folders, including the Inbox, Drafts, Sent Items, Deleted Items, Junk E-mail, News Feed, Outbox, RSS Feeds, and Search folders. Icons in the Inbox help you identify mail that is read, unread, has been forwarded or replied to, or has threaded messages. A **threaded message** includes all e-mails that discuss a common subject. Message threading allows you to navigate through a group of messages, seeing all replies and forwards from all recipients. You can also set Follow-Up flags for messages.

2. **Click the Arrange By button in the Inbox**

   The menu opens as shown in Figure B-5. You see the many ways of sorting, grouping, and arranging e-mail messages. You can determine how you view the e-mail in any folder. Options include by Date, Conversation, Categories, Subject, Attachments, and Importance. Create mail folders for projects, people, or ideas. You can use Outlook to quickly **filter**, or show a specific group of your e-mail messages, based on specific criteria, such as who sent you a message. Search your messages for keywords by typing a search term in the Search Inbox box and clicking the Search button.

3. **Click the File tab on the Ribbon, verify that Info is selected in the Navigation Pane, then click the Manage Rules & Alerts button**

   The Rules and Alerts dialog box opens, as shown in Figure B-6. You can specify how you want your mail from specific senders or other criteria to sort as it arrives.

4. **Click Cancel to close the Rules and Alerts dialog box, click Options in the Navigation Pane, then click Mail in the left pane of the Outlook Options dialog box**

   The Mail options are shown in Figure B-7. You can set options for how messages are formatted and how mail looks and sounds when it arrives. Set how Outlook handles forwarding, replying to, sending, tracking, and formatting messages.

5. **Click Cancel, click the Home tab, then click the Junk button in the Delete group**

   By specifying safe senders and blocked senders, you can be sure that the e-mail you get is the e-mail you want to receive. You can add a person's e-mail address to your Safe Senders list. If e-mail comes in that you know is offensive add the source address to the Blocked Senders list.

6. **Click the Inbox for your account, click the View tab, click the Show as Conversations check box to select it, click All Folders, click the Change View button in the Current View group, click Single, click the Change View button, click Preview, click the Change View button, then click Compact**

   You can control how the Inbox appears by using the View options.

FIGURE B-4: Viewing Inbox arranged by date

Search box

Arrange By button

Default mail folders

Replied to message

Forwarded message

Assigned category

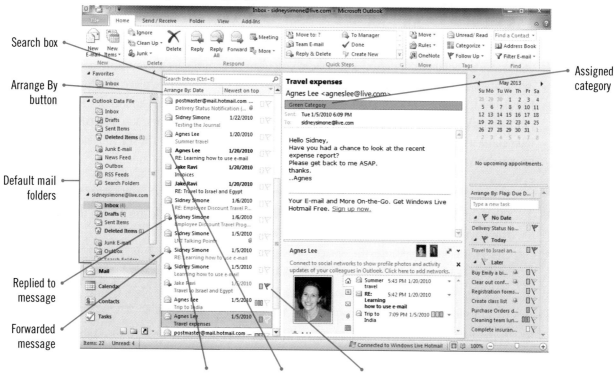

Read message   Unread message   Follow Up flag

FIGURE B-5: Arrange By options

Arrange By button

FIGURE B-6: Rules and Alerts dialog box

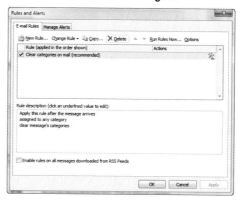

FIGURE B-7: Outlook Mail options

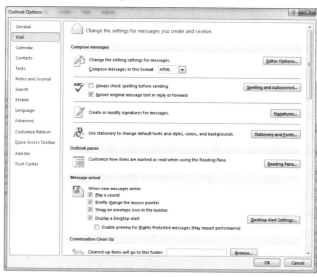

Adding Contacts

Contacts in Microsoft Outlook let you manage all your business and personal contact information. When you create a contact for a person with whom you want to communicate, you store general and detailed information about that person in fields. A **field** is an area that stores one piece of information, such as a first name or an e-mail address. Once you create a contact, you can quickly address letters, locate a phone number, make a call, send a meeting request, assign a task, or e-mail a message. You can sort, group, and filter contacts by any field. You can also easily share contacts with others. █████ You learn about Contacts so you can store all the contact information for employees and clients in Outlook.

STEPS

QUICK TIP

Click the Normal or Cards Only buttons on the status bar to change the view. Use the Zoom slider to increase or decrease the size and number of cards that fit on a screen.

1. **Click Contacts in the Navigation Pane, click the View tab, click the To-Do Bar button in the Layout group, then click Off**

   The Navigation Pane changes to Contacts view, and the To-Do Bar closes. Figure B-8 shows several completed contacts in a Contacts folder in Business Card view.

2. **Click the Home tab, then click the New Contact button in the New group**

   You enter information for a new contact in each field in the Contact window.

3. **Type your name as the contact name in the Full Name text box, press [Tab], type Quest Specialty Travel (QST) in the Company text box, press [Tab], type Human Resources Assistant in the Job title text box, then type your E-mail address, Business, Home, and Mobile telephone numbers in the appropriate text boxes**

   If you do not enter a first and last name in the Full Name text box, the Check Full Name dialog box opens so you can enter the full name for the contact. Determine how Outlook files each contact by clicking the File as list arrow in the Contact window, then click by first name, last name, company, or job title.

TROUBLE

If the Location Information dialog box opens, enter your local area code, click OK, then click OK in the Phone and Modem dialog box.

4. **Click the Addresses list arrow, click Business if necessary, click the This is the mailing address check box to select it if necessary, then type your address in the Address text box**

   You can store up to three addresses in the Address text box. Choose Business, Home, or Other from the Addresses list, then type the address in the Address text box. If Outlook can't identify an address component that you type in the Address text box, the Check Address dialog box opens for you to verify the component.

5. **Click the MapIt button in the Contact card**

   If your computer is connected to the Internet, a browser window opens and shows the location on a map.

6. **Close the browser window if it is open, click the Business Card button in the Options group to open the Edit Business Card dialog box, click Full Name, Company, Job Title, Business Phone, and Business Address in the Fields list to view the information for each field in the Edit window on the right, then click Cancel**

   You use the Edit Business Card dialog box to view and edit, when necessary, contact information.

7. **Click the Picture button in the Options group, then click Add Picture**

   You use the Add Contact Picture dialog box to navigate to select the photo, and then click Open.

QUICK TIP

When you create a new Outlook item, such as a task, appointment, or note, you can link it to the contact or contacts to which it relates.

8. **Add a photo if you have one, or click Cancel, then click the Details button in the Show group on the Contact card**

   You can enter a contact's detailed information, including the contact's department, profession, assistant's name, birthday, anniversary, spouse or partner's name, or even the contact's nickname.

9. **Click the Click to Expand the People Pane button ▲ in the Contact card, view the Social Networking options, click the Click to collapse the People Pane button ▼ in the People Pane, then click the Save & Close button in the Actions group**

   Figure B-9 shows a Contact card with a photo as a business card.

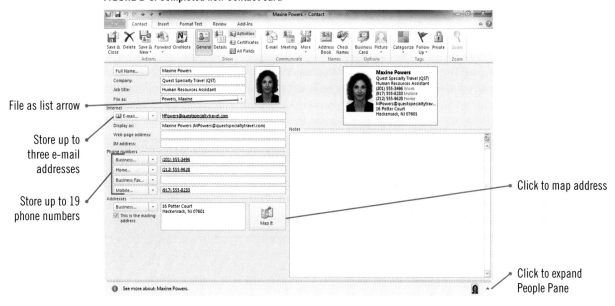

FIGURE B-8: **Contacts**

Business Card View button

New Contact button

Contact folders

Contacts

Click to open e-mail address book

Jump to cards by clicking letter for contact last name

Normal button — Cards Only button — No To-Do Bar button

FIGURE B-9: **Completed new Contact card**

File as list arrow

Store up to three e-mail addresses

Store up to 19 phone numbers

Click to map address

Click to expand People Pane

Creating a Contact Group

You can create a subset of your Contacts folder by creating a Contact Group. Contact Groups work in the same way as distribution lists. A **Contact Group** is a subset of the people in your Contacts folder, grouped together by e-mail addresses. You can create a Contact Group based on any criteria, such as all contacts that live in New York City, all contacts that are clients, all contacts that work for a specific company, or even a combination of such criteria. Once the Contact Group is created, you can send a message, task request, or meeting request to everyone in the group with a single click. To create a Contact Group from the Contacts module, click the Home tab, then click the New Contact Group button in the New group. In the Contact Group window that opens, enter a descriptive name for the group in the Name box. Click the Add Members button in the Members group to select Members from Outlook Contacts or from the address book. You can also add new e-mail contacts. Click the Save & Close button when you are done adding members.

Managing Appointments

The **Calendar** in Microsoft Outlook provides a convenient, effective way to manage your appointments. Calendar is the electronic equivalent of your desk calendar or pocket calendar. Calendar defines an **appointment** as an activity that does not involve inviting other people or scheduling resources; a **meeting** as an activity you invite people to or reserve resources for; and an **event** as an activity that lasts 24 hours or longer. You can specify the subject and location of the activity and its start and end times. You can also ensure that you do not forget the activity by having Outlook sound and display a reminder for you before the start of the activity. When you create an activity, Outlook notifies you if the new activity conflicts with, or is adjacent to, another scheduled activity. You can set up recurring appointments or events by specifying the recurrence, such as every week, month, or any period of time, and when the recurrence ends. People in your group or company can each have their own calendars. To help with managing time, you can view more than one calendar side by side in the Outlook window. ▨▨▨▨ You will use Outlook to manage the schedule for the Human Resources department

STEPS

TROUBLE
If more than one calendar is open, remove the check marks to close all but your calendar.

1. **Click Calendar in the Navigation Pane, click the Week button in the Arrange group, then click the the Month button in the Arrange group**

   The calendar, as shown in Figure B-10 in Week view, can be viewed either by day, work week, week, or month. The To-Do Bar, if open, shows the current month in the Date Navigator; if the To-Do Bar is closed, the Date Navigator appears in the Navigation Pane. You can use the Date Navigator in the To-Do Bar or Navigation Pane to quickly view specific dates. Dates with appointments or events appear in bold in the Date Navigator. Tasks for each day appear below the calendar so you can see what tasks are due on each day.

2. **Click any date next week in your calendar, click the Home tab if it is not selected, then click the New Appointment button in the New Group**

   An untitled Appointment window opens. See Figure B-11. You can specify the subject and location and categorize the appointment with a specific color. You enter recurring appointments once, then set a recurrence pattern. You can choose how you want the appointment to appear on your calendar, as Free, Tentative, Busy, or Out of Office, and a graphic bar appears on the left side of the appointment.

QUICK TIP
To quickly enter an appointment, click the time slot in the calendar, then type the information.

3. **Type Review Travel Agendas in the Subject text box, type Conference Room A in the Location text box, click the Start time list arrow, click the date that is one week from the date you clicked in Step 2, click the Start time list arrow, click 9:00 AM, click the Reminder list arrow in the Options group on the Ribbon, then click 1 day**

   If this were a one-time meeting, you could click the Save & Close button in the Actions group and the appointment would be set. Reminders appear with a reminder icon 🔔 in the appointment.

4. **Click the Recurrence button in the Options group, review the default recurrence options shown in Figure B-12, click the End after option button, type 52 in the occurrences text box, click OK, then click the Save & Close button in the Actions group**

   The Appointment window closes. This is a recurring event that will display on your calendar each week for 52 weeks. Recurring events or appointments appear with the 🔁 icon.

5. **Click anywhere in the calendar, click the Home tab, click the Day button in the Arrange group, click the Work Week button, click the Week button, then click the Forward button ▶ in the calendar three times**

   You can view the calendar by day, week, or month. In all calendar views, click the Time Scale button in the Arrangement group on the View tab to change the level of detail of the days shown.

QUICK TIP
When viewing the calendar, if you click a meeting or appointment, the details appear in the Reading Pane.

6. **On the Home tab, in the Go To group, click the Today button to return to today's date**

7. **In the New group, click the New Meeting button, in the Show group click the Scheduling button, then click the Untitled Meeting Close button ▨✕▨ on the title bar**

   The calendar can check the availability of all the invitees and resources for the meetings you want to set up.

FIGURE B-10: Calendar for a week

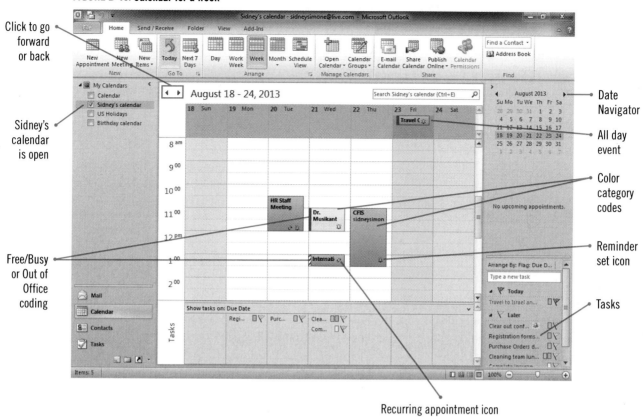

Click to go forward or back

Sidney's calendar is open

Free/Busy or Out of Office coding

Date Navigator

All day event

Color category codes

Reminder set icon

Tasks

Recurring appointment icon

FIGURE B-11: New Appointment window

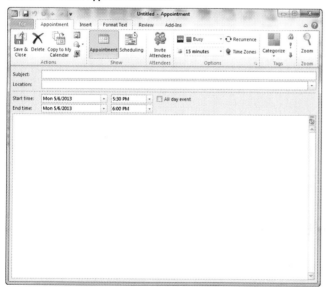

FIGURE B-12: Appointment Recurrence dialog box

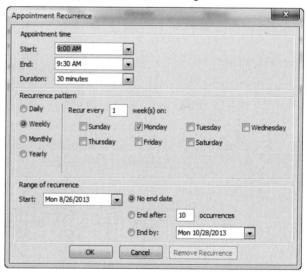

Sending electronic business cards

You can send contact information over the Internet easily with Outlook. If you know someone has Outlook, you can send a contact business card. In Contacts view, click the contact you want to send, then, on the Home tab, click the Forward Contact button in the Share group. You can choose to send the card as a business card or an Outlook contact, and you can forward the card as a text message. If you send it as a business card, you will send the contact as a .vcf electronic file to someone via e-mail.

Managing Tasks

Tasks in Outlook is an electronic to-do list. When you have something you need to do, you can enter it in Tasks. Each task has a subject, a start and due date, and a description. You can also assign a priority to a task. You can mark your progress on tasks by percentage complete, and you can have Outlook create status summary reports in e-mail messages and then send the summary to anyone on a task update list. Tasks can also have reminders. When you are in an Outlook module other than Tasks, your tasks appear at the bottom of the To-Do Bar, if it is open. You can also view the tasks that are due on each date in the Calendar. Similar to meetings and events, tasks can recur. You can also assign a flag and category to each task to help you organize your tasks. ▨▨▨ A week from tomorrow, the main conference room at the office is being painted, and you have to prepare the room. You enter the task in Outlook to keep track of it.

STEPS

1. **Click Tasks in the Navigation Pane**

2. **Click the New Task button in the New group**

   The new untitled Task window opens.

3. **Type Clear out conference room in the Subject text box, click the Start date list arrow, click the date that is one week from today, click the Priority list arrow, click High, click the Reminder check box to select it, click the Reminder date list arrow, then click the date that is one week from yesterday**

4. **Click the Categorize button in the Tags group, click Purple Category (or the category that is purple, if it has a different name), click No in the Rename Category dialog box if necessary, click the Follow Up button in the Tags group, then click Next Week**

   The completed task looks like Figure B-13.

5. **Click the Save & Close button in the Actions group**

   You can arrange your tasks in several different ways, such as by Date, Category, Start Date, Due Date, Folder, Type, or Importance. Click a column header in the task list to change sort order. Tasks can also be viewed in many ways by clicking the View tab and using the options in the Arrangement and Current View groups. Click the Change View button in the Current View group to see view options. Figure B-14 shows Tasks in Simple List view. A few existing tasks appear in the window (your screen may be different).

6. **On the Home tab, in the New group click the New Task button to open the Untitled Task window, then click the Assign Task button in the Manage Task group**

   You can assign tasks to another person and have Outlook automatically update you on the status of the task completion. To assign a task, you fill in the e-mail address of the person to whom you are assigning the task, complete the task details, and then click Send.

7. **Click the Cancel Assignment button in the Manage Task group, close the Untitled Task window, then click No to saving changes**

8. **Click Calendar in the Navigation Pane, click the Today button in the Go To group if the calendar does not open to today, then scroll to next week in the calendar or Date Navigator or until you see the new task you just entered**

   To coordinate your tasks and your appointments, the task list from Tasks is displayed in the Tasks section below the calendar. The task you just created should appear under the calendar for next week. You can specify how tasks are organized in the To-Do Bar.

9. **Click the Arrange By button above the tasks in the To-Do Bar, then click Start Date**

   To schedule time to complete a task, drag a task from the To-Do Bar to a time block in the Calendar. Any changes you make to a task are reflected in both the To-Do Bar in Calendar and the task list in Tasks.

FIGURE B-13: Task information entered

Task subject

Details

Category

Reminder date

High priority

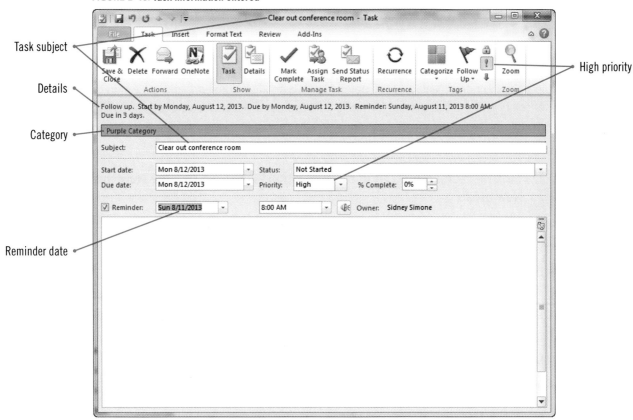

FIGURE B-14: Tasks in Simple List view

Click to enter a new task

Click to change sort order

Change View button

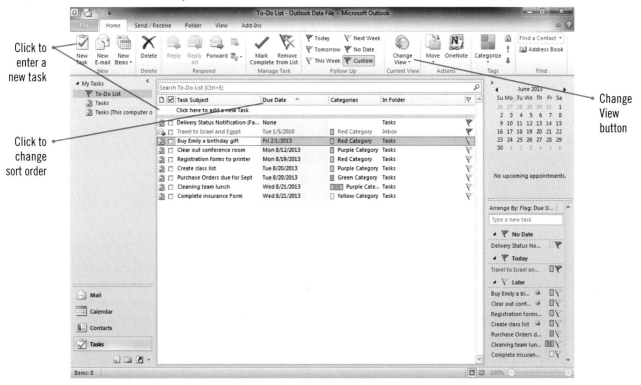

Creating Notes

Notes in Microsoft Outlook is the electronic version of the sticky notes or Post-It™ notes you buy at your local stationery store. Notes created in Outlook are a convenient way to quickly jot down a reminder or an idea. You can group and organize notes, like tasks and appointments, and can assign categories, contacts, or colors to them. You can also forward a note to share an idea with a colleague. ![palette icon] You use the Notes module in Outlook to quickly write down an idea concerning a new employee at Quest Specialty Travel.

STEPS

1. **Click the** Notes button ![icon] **in the Navigation Pane, then click the** New Note button **in the New group**

   The Note window opens. See Figure B-15. You type the note directly in the Note window. The note should begin with a meaningful phrase so that the Notes list displays a clear descriptive title for it.

2. **Type** Maxine Powers-File new health forms with insurance company

QUICK TIP

If a note is covering an area of the window you want to view, click the title bar of the note and drag it to a new location.

3. **Click the** Note icon **in the upper-left corner of the Note window to open a menu, then point to** Categorize

   See Figure B-16. You can color code each note, assign a contact to the note, and forward or print the note. Notes are date- and time-stamped at the time they are created.

4. **Click** Purple Category **(or the name of the purple category, if necessary)**

   The Navigation Pane provides many options for viewing the notes in order to organize them the way you want. If you want to turn a note into an appointment or meeting, you drag the note from the Notes window to the Calendar button in the Navigation Pane. A new Appointment window opens with the details from the note filled in the appropriate fields. If you drag the note to the Tasks button in the Navigation Pane, a new task window opens and you can specify a due date and other details.

QUICK TIP

To quickly copy a note, drag the note while you press [Ctrl].

5. **Close the note**

   You can copy, move, or delete notes. You can also organize them in many different ways to best meet your needs. Right-click the Notes area to open the shortcut menu with options in a Notes window with several notes. Each note has a category assignment. See Figure B-17.

Customizing Outlook Today

When Outlook Today is open, you can see what is happening in the Calendar, Tasks, and Messages modules for the day. To open Outlook Today, click the Shortcuts button in the Navigation Pane, then click Outlook Today in the Navigation Pane. Outlook Today shows your appointments over a range of time in the Calendar section. It also displays your tasks in one convenient place. You can also choose to show from one to seven days of appointments in the Calendar section, and you can sort your tasks in Outlook Today by Importance, Due Date, Creation Time, or Start Date and in ascending or descending order. If you use Outlook for e-mail, Outlook Today displays how many messages are in your Inbox, Drafts, RSS Feeds, and Outbox folders. You can also add or delete folders from the Messages folder list. To customize Outlook Today, view the Outlook Today page, click the Customize Outlook Today link to the right of the date in Outlook Today, and set the options to fit your personal style and work habits. In the Customize Outlook Today Pane, you can decide to go directly to Outlook Today when Outlook opens, if it does not open automatically. Pick a different visual appearance for Outlook Today from an available list. Click the Save Changes link in the Customize Outlook Today Pane to save any changes you make.

FIGURE B-15: Create a new note

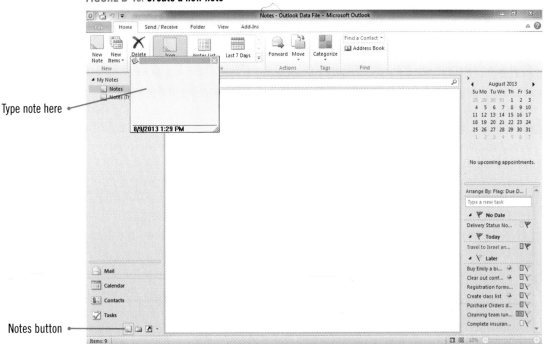

Type note here

Notes button

FIGURE B-16: Notes menu with Category options

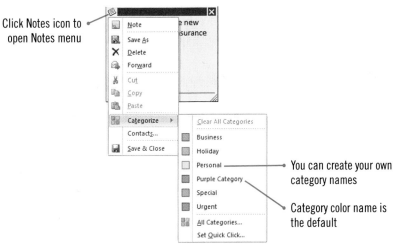

Click Notes icon to open Notes menu

You can create your own category names

Category color name is the default

FIGURE B-17: Notes in Icon view

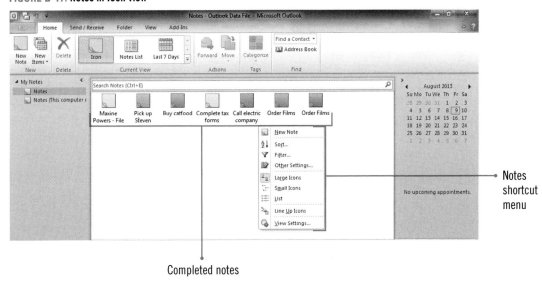

Completed notes

Notes shortcut menu

Using the Journal

The **Journal** in Outlook is a way to provide a trail of your activities within Microsoft Office. If you turn the Journal on, you can see a timeline of any calls, messages, appointments, or tasks. The Journal also tracks all documents, spreadsheets, databases, presentations, or any Office file that you specify. The Journal may not have been on when you created a spreadsheet or document that you want to be recorded in the Journal. But you can add it to the Journal. Use Windows Explorer or the desktop to locate the file or item you want to record, then drag the item to the Journal and select the options you want for the entry. You use the Journal to help assign documents to contacts.

STEPS

1. **Click the Configure buttons button ▼ in the Navigation Pane, point to Add or Remove Buttons, click Journal, click the Journal button 📓, then click Yes in the message box to turn on the Journal**

   To turn on the Journal, you specify the Journal options, such as which items to track, in the Journal Options dialog box, shown in Figure B-18. The Journal is displayed as a timeline on your screen. Any activities that have been specified to be tracked appear for each day as icons. You can scroll through the Journal to get an overview of your activities. You can sort or group the activities in the Journal. If you want to recall an event, the Journal is a great tool; you can see any documents that may have been created on a specific day. The Journal folder contains shortcuts to the activities that have been recorded.

2. **Click the E-mail Message check box in the Automatically record these items box, click the check box next to your name in the For these contacts list, then click OK**

3. **Click Mail in the Navigation Pane, click the New E-Mail button in the New group, then send yourself a test message with the subject Testing the Journal and the body of the message I am sending this message to test the Journal.**

4. **Click the Journal button 📓 on the Naviation Pane, and view the Journal entry, as shown in Figure B-19**

5. **Click the Journal Entry button in the New group, then click the Entry type list arrow**

   A new Journal Entry window opens. You can create journal entries for activities such as phone calls or tasks using this dialog box. There are many different journal entries you can manually add to your journal.

6. **Click the Entry type list arrow to close the list, then in the Journal Entry window, click the Delete button in the Actions group**

   To turn off the Journal, you have to clear the Journal Options dialog box.

7. **Click the File tab, click Options, click the Notes and Journal tab, click Journal Options, then click to remove the check marks from the E-mail Message check box and from your contact name**

8. **Click OK to close the Journal Options dialog box, then click OK to close the Outlook Options dialog box**

9. **Click the Configure Buttons button ▼ in the Navigation Pane, point to Add or Remove Buttons, then click Journal**

FIGURE B-18: Journal Options dialog box

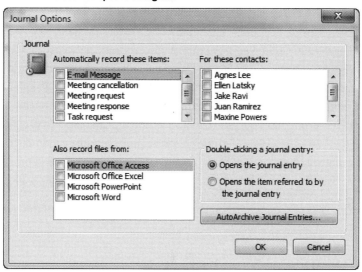

FIGURE B-19: The Journal

Journal active

Journal button

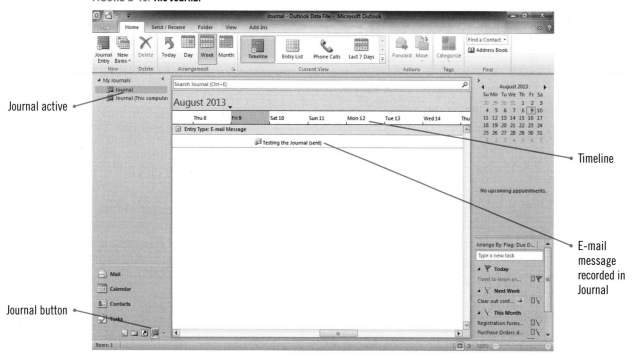

Timeline

E-mail message recorded in Journal

Applying Categories

You use categories in Outlook to tag items so you can track and organize them by specific criteria. Outlook comes with color categories that are set by default. You can rename the colors as needed. For example, red can be urgent, blue can be business, and green can be personal. By assigning color categories to contacts, tasks, appointments, notes, or any item in Outlook, you can quickly review all items assigned to a specific category by reviewing the color. You can filter or sort by category. If you change your Contacts view to List view and then click the Categories button in the Arrangement section of the View tab, you can see your contacts clearly by category. QST wants to use color to help organize information about its contacts and staff. Eventually, you will set up a system to assign colors to contacts and staff based on region.

STEPS

1. **Click Contacts in the Navigation Pane**

2. **Click your Contact card, then click the Categorize button in the Tags group**
   Outlook comes with six predefined color categories: Purple, Orange, Blue, Green, Red, and Yellow.

3. **Click Purple Category (or the name of the purple category, if its name has been changed)**
   Your Contact card is now assigned the color purple. If you open the card, or if you view contacts as a list, you can see the color bar. You can assign more than one category to a contact.

4. **Click Calendar in the Navigation Pane, click the Forward button ▶ to scroll to next week, click the Review Travel Agendas appointment, click the Categorize button in the Tags group, then click Purple Category (or the category's name)**
   The appointment is also assigned the color purple.

5. **Click Contacts in the Navigation Pane, click the View tab, click the Change View button in the Current view group, click the List button, then click the Categories button in the Arrangement group**
   The contacts are grouped by category, as shown in Figure B-20. You can rename categories to be meaningful while retaining the color coding.

6. **Make sure a Contact card is selected, click the Home tab, click the Categorize button in the Tags group, then click All Categories to open the Color Categories dialog box, as shown in Figure B-21**

QUICK TIP
If you are working on a shared computer, such as in a lab setting, repeat Steps 6 and 7 to change the category name back to Purple Category.

7. **Click Purple Category (or the category's name), click Rename, type HR Assistant as the new name, then click OK**
   The name of the purple category changes to "HR Assistant" in the list of contacts by category. As you work on other applications at your computer, you can leave Outlook open so you can refer to your contacts, be reminded of appointments, and track entries in the Journal. However, at the end of the day, it is good practice to close all applications and shut down the computer.

8. **Click the File tab, then click Exit to exit Outlook**

FIGURE B-20: Contacts grouped by category

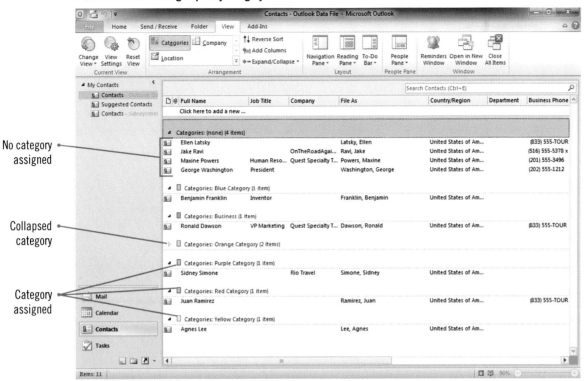

No category assigned

Collapsed category

Category assigned

FIGURE B-21: Color Categories dialog box

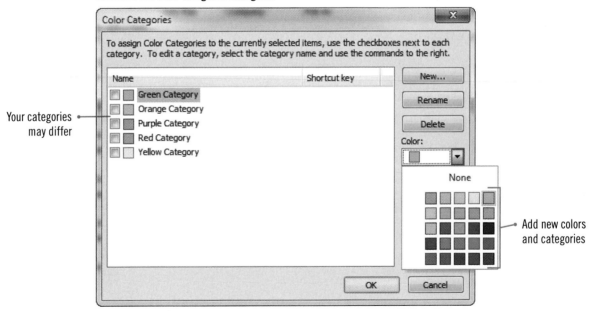

Your categories may differ

Add new colors and categories

Coordinating calendars

Calendar can check the availability of all the people and resources for the meetings you want to set up.

Once you select a meeting time and location, you can send invitations in meeting requests by entering contact names in the To text box, then clicking the Send button. The meeting request arrives in the invitee's Inbox with buttons to Accept, Reject, or Request a change directly in the e-mail message. If an invitee accepts the invitation, a positive e-mail reply is sent back to you, and Outlook posts the meeting automatically to the invitee's calendar. If you share calendars through a network, you can click the Open a Shared Calendar link in the Navigation Pane to view the calendars of your colleagues. To send a copy of a time period in your calendar to someone through e-mail, click the Send a Calendar via E-mail link in the Navigation Pane, adjust the options in the Send a Calendar via E-mail dialog box, click OK, then address and send the e-mail.

Practice

For current SAM information, including versions and content details, visit SAM Central (http://www.cengage.com/samcentral). If you have a SAM user profile, you may have access to hands-on instruction, practice, and assessment of the skills covered in this unit. Since various versions of SAM are supported throughout the life of this text, check with your instructor for the correct instructions and URL/Web site for accessing assignments.

Concepts Review

Label each element of the Calendar window shown in Figure B-22.

FIGURE B-22

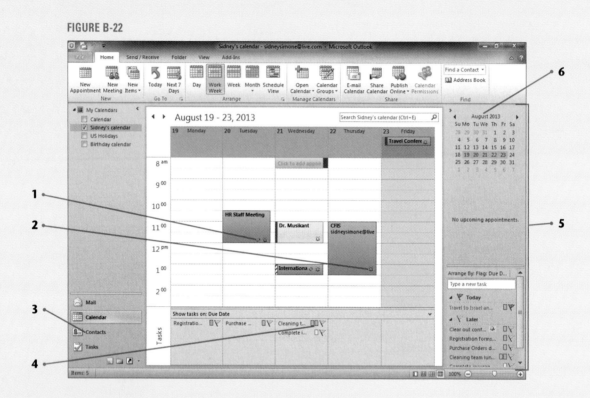

Match each term with the statement that best describes it.

7. Notes

8. Tasks

9. E-mail

10. Calendar

11. Journal

a. Manage a to-do list

b. Keep and track appointments

c. Send and receive messages

d. Track e-mail, documents, and activities

e. Jot down ideas or reminders

Select the best answer from the list of choices.

12. **Which of the following is *not* available in Outlook?**
    - **a.** Mail
    - **b.** Paint
    - **c.** Calendar
    - **d.** Notes

13. **To color code your appointments, meetings, contacts, and events, use _____.**
    - **a.** Flags
    - **b.** Journal
    - **c.** Categories
    - **d.** Timeline

14. **If you want to send an e-mail to the same 15 people every time, you should create and use a(n) _____.**
    - **a.** Category
    - **b.** Contact Group
    - **c.** Address book
    - **d.** Cluster

15. **To see the Contact picture you added to a Contact card, use the _____ view.**
    - **a.** Business Card
    - **b.** Card
    - **c.** List
    - **d.** Graphic

16. **The difference between an appointment and an event is that _____.**
    - **a.** an event cannot recur
    - **b.** an appointment lasts less than 12 hours
    - **c.** an event lasts 24 hours or more
    - **d.** you cannot categorize an event

17. **Which of the following is *not* visible on the To-Do Bar?**
    - **a.** Date Navigator
    - **b.** An appointment for today
    - **c.** Tasks due today
    - **d.** E-mail in the Inbox

18. **If an appointment happens every Tuesday, you should set a _____ when setting up the appointment.**
    - **a.** recurrence
    - **b.** reminder
    - **c.** category
    - **d.** journal entry

19. **When you enter an incomplete address that doesn't meet the field requirments in a new Contact card, Outlook _____.**
    - **a.** maps the address to help you find it
    - **b.** leaves the address as is
    - **c.** closes the dialog box and cancels the contact
    - **d.** opens the Check Address dialog box

20. **When you enter an incomplete name that doesn't meet the field requirments in a new Contact card, Outlook _____.**
    - **a.** opens the Check Full Name dialog box
    - **b.** leaves the name as is
    - **c.** closes the dialog box and cancels the contact
    - **d.** offers a list of possible suggestions

Skills Review

1. **Start Outlook.**
   a. Start Outlook.
   b. Arrange the Outlook window so that the Navigation Pane is in Normal view with the folder list on the left side of the screen and the To-Do Bar on the right side.
   c. If there is any mail in the Inbox, click a message and view the message in the Reading Pane.
   d. Click each tab on the Ribbon and view the different command buttons.
   e. Click the Home tab on the Ribbon.

2. **Organize e-mail.**
   a. View the Inbox.
   b. View the e-mail in the Inbox by Sender, view the Inbox by Size, then view the e-mail in the Inbox by Date (Conversations), with the most recent on top. (*Hint*: Sender is From on the list.)
   c. If you have any messages in your Inbox, select the message, expand the People Pane, review the contents, then collapse the People Pane.

Skills Review (continued)

d. Open a New Message window and write an e-mail message to your instructor or a friend. Include an address in the Cc box, then type **Study group plans** as the subject of the message. As the body of the message, enter the message shown in Figure B-23.

e. Send the message.

f. Open the Sent Items folder, review the e-mail options, then return to the Inbox.

FIGURE B-23

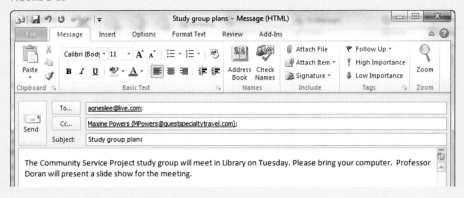

3. Add contacts.

a. Open Contacts.

b. Open a new untitled Contact window.

c. Create a new contact using the information in Figure B-24.

d. If you have a photo or any picture, add it to the Contact card.

e. If you are connected to the Internet, click the MapIt button and locate the address on a map.

f. Save and close the contact.

FIGURE B-24

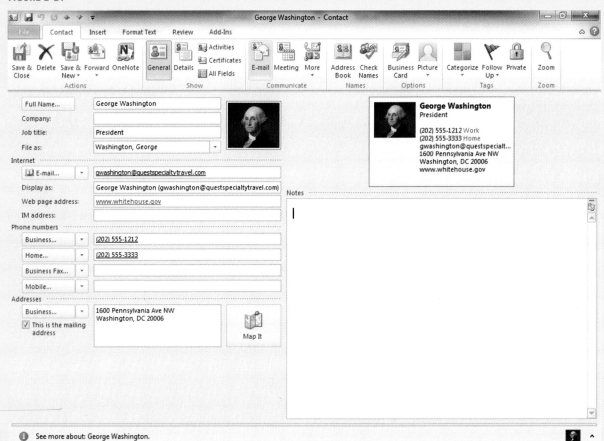

Skills Review (continued)

4. Manage appointments.

   a. Open Calendar.

   b. View the calendar by full week.

   c. View the calendar for today.

   d. Create a new appointment for next week for a two-and-a-half hour lunch meeting with Ruth, Maureen, and Janice at noon in the Stardust Diner. Set a reminder for four hours. See Figure B-25.

   e. Save and close the appointment.

FIGURE B-25

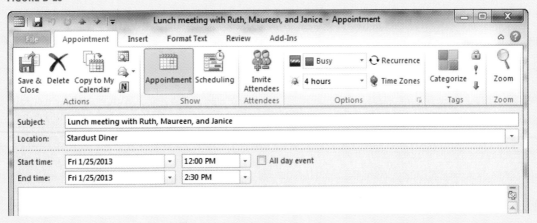

5. Manage tasks.

   a. Open Tasks.

   b. Create a new task that starts next month.

   c. The subject of the task is **Buy Emily a birthday gift**.

   d. Assign the task to the Red category.

   e. Set a reminder for early morning one week before the task is due. See Figure B-26.

   f. Save and close the task.

   g. View the task list in Simple List and Detailed List views.

FIGURE B-26

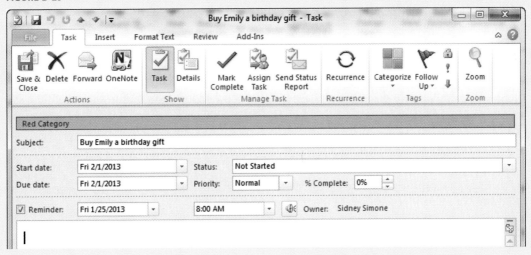

Skills Review (continued)

6. Create notes.

  a. Open Notes.

  b. Create a new note with the following text: **Call town hall about the new library hours.**

  c. Categorize the note in the Blue category. See Figure B-27.

  d. Close the note.

7. Use the Journal.

  a. Turn on the Journal.

  b. In the Journal Options dialog box, to have the Journal track your e-mail messages, click the E-mail Message check box in the Automatically record these items box and the check box next to your own name in the "For these contacts."

  c. Send yourself an e-mail message.

  d. Open the Journal to view the Journal entry.

  e. Open the Journal Options dialog box, deselect the E-mail Message check box in the Automatically record these items box, then deselect the check box next to your name to turn tracking off.

  f. Close the Journal Options dialog box.

8. Apply categories.

  a. Open Contacts, then assign the Green category to your Contact card.

  b. Assign a category to the lunch appointment that you created in Step 4.

  c. Assign a second category to the task you created in Step 5.

  d. View Contacts by category.

  e. View the tasks by category.

  f. Exit Outlook.

FIGURE B-27

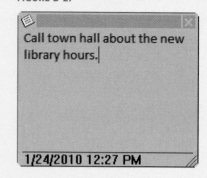

Independent Challenge 1

As manager of a local pet store, your job is to develop a contact list of all customers that come into the store. The list will be used to send direct mail for future promotions. You created a form for customers to complete so that you can gather their contact information. The information includes first and last name, mailing address, e-mail address, and at least one phone number. Each week, you select one customer from the list of new names to receive a small prize package. You need to create the contact list in Outlook and use Outlook to schedule the weekly prize giveaway.

  a. Open Contacts in Outlook, and then create five new Contact cards. Use your friends' information or make up fictitious names and contact information.

  b. Create two notes, each in the Blue category, that remind you of an event in the store.

  c. Create a recurring appointment on each Thursday for the next two months to select a winner from the list of new names.

  d. Enter two new tasks in the task list. One task is for you to review the employee compensation package, and the other task is for you to review the utility bills. Each task should have a start date of next week, a high priority, and be in the Yellow category.

  e. View the Calendar with the To-Do Bar open.

  f. Exit Outlook.

Independent Challenge 2

Outlook is an integrated information management system that stores information in folders specific to the type of information stored. Outlook stores e-mail in Mail folders, contacts in Contact folders, and so on. You can create new folders for specific types of information and view them in the folders list. You can also transfer one type of item to another, for example, you can drag a task to the Calendar to create an appointment. The integration of the different types of information is what makes Outlook so powerful. You are going to move items from one Outlook module to another to see how easily you can integrate information.

a. Open Mail in Outlook, then drag an e-mail message from the Inbox to Tasks in the Navigation Pane to create a new task. In a word-processing document or on a piece of paper, explain what happens. What elements of the mail message are entered in which task fields?

b. Drag an e-mail message from the Inbox to Notes in the Navigation Pane, then explain what happens.

c. Open the Calendar, drag an existing appointment from the Calendar to Tasks in the Navigation Pane, then explain what happens.

d. Drag the same appointment to Mail in the Navigation Pane.

e. View the Contacts list in Business Card view. Drag a Contact card from the Contacts list to Calendar in the Navigation Pane, then explain what happens.

Advanced Challenge Exercise

- Open an existing contact, click the Categorize button, then click All Categories.
- Rename the Purple and Red categories to a name of your choice, close the Color Categories dialog box, then assign the contact to both categories.
- Click the Details button in the Show group on the Contact tab, then enter at least two details in the fields.
- Save and close the contact.

f. View the Contacts list in Business Card view. Drag a Contact card from the Contacts list to Mail in the Navigation Pane, then explain what happens.

g. Exit Outlook.

Visual Workshop

Start Outlook. First, create a new contact, as shown in Figure B-28, using any photo you want. Create an appointment as shown in Figure B-29, using a weekday in the next two weeks as the date for the appointment. Finally, using the same date as for the appointment, create a task, as shown in Figure B-30. Note that the dates in the figures will differ from those on your screen.

FIGURE B-28

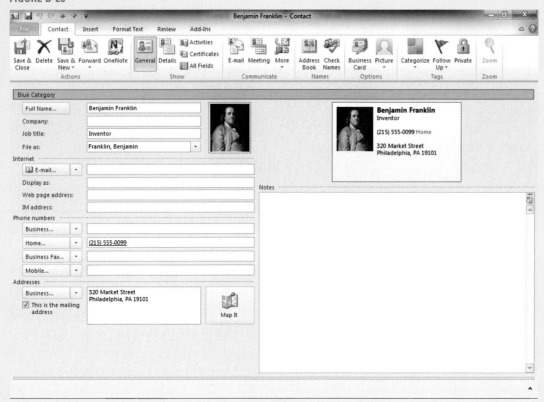

FIGURE B-29

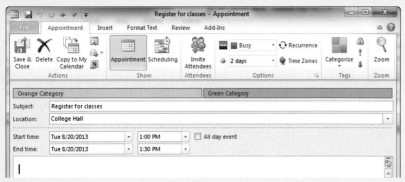

FIGURE B-30

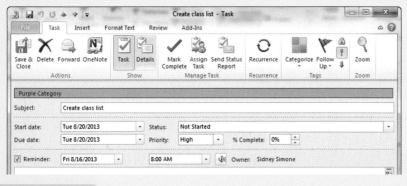

Working with Windows Live and Office Web Apps

If the computer you are using has an active Internet connection, you can go to the Microsoft Windows Live Web site and access a wide variety of services and Web applications. For example, you can check your e-mail through Windows Live, network with your friends and coworkers, and use SkyDrive to store and share files. From SkyDrive, you can also use Office Web Apps to create and edit Word, PowerPoint, Excel, and OneNote files, even when you are using a computer that does not have Office 2010 installed. ▓▓▓▓ You work in the Vancouver branch of Quest Specialty Travel. Your supervisor, Mary Lou Jacobs, asks you to explore Windows Live and learn how she can use SkyDrive and Office Web Apps to work with her files online.

(*Note*: SkyDrive and Office Web Apps are dynamic Web pages, and might change over time, including the way they are organized and how commands are performed. The steps and figures in this appendix were accurate at the time this book was published.)

OBJECTIVES

Explore how to work online from Windows Live

Obtain a Windows Live ID and sign in to Windows Live

Upload files to Windows Live

Work with the PowerPoint Web App

Create folders and organize files on SkyDrive

Add people to your network and share files

Work with the Excel Web App

Exploring How to Work Online from Windows Live

You can use your Web browser to upload your files to Windows Live from any computer connected to the Internet. You can work on the files right in your Web browser using Office Web Apps and share your files with people in your Windows Live network.  You review the concepts and services related to working online from Windows Live.

DETAILS

- **What is Windows Live?**

  Windows Live is a collection of services and Web applications that you can use to help you be more productive both personally and professionally. For example, you can use Windows Live to send and receive e-mail, to chat with friends via instant messaging, to share photos, to create a blog, and to store and edit files using SkyDrive. Table WEB-1 describes the services available on Windows Live. Windows Live is a free service that you sign up for. When you sign up, you receive a Windows Live ID, which you use to sign in to Windows Live. When you work with files on Windows Live, you are cloud computing.

- **What is Cloud Computing?**

  The term **cloud computing** refers to the process of working with files online in a Web browser. When you save files to SkyDrive on Windows Live, you are saving your files to an online location. SkyDrive is like having a personal hard drive in the cloud.

- **What is SkyDrive?**

  SkyDrive is an online storage and file sharing service. With a Windows Live account, you receive access to your own SkyDrive, which is your personal storage area on the Internet. On your SkyDrive, you are given space to store up to 25 GB of data online. Each file can be a maximum size of 50 MB. You can also use SkyDrive to access Office Web Apps, which you use to create and edit files created in Word, OneNote, PowerPoint, and Excel online in your Web browser.

- **Why use Windows Live and SkyDrive?**

  On Windows Live, you use SkyDrive to access additional storage for your files. You don't have to worry about backing up your files to a memory stick or other storage device that could be lost or damaged. Another advantage of storing your files on SkyDrive is that you can access your files from any computer that has an active Internet connection. Figure WEB-1 shows the SkyDrive Web page that appears when accessed from a Windows Live account. From SkyDrive, you can also access Office Web Apps.

- **What are Office Web Apps?**

  Office Web Apps are versions of Microsoft Word, Excel, PowerPoint, and OneNote that you can access online from your SkyDrive. An Office Web App does not include all of the features and functions included with the full Office version of its associated application. However, you can use the Office Web App from any computer that is connected to the Internet, even if Microsoft Office 2010 is not installed on that computer.

- **How do SkyDrive and Office Web Apps work together?**

  You can create a file in Office 2010 using Word, Excel, PowerPoint, or OneNote and then upload the file to your SkyDrive. You can then open the Office file saved to SkyDrive and edit it using your Web browser and the corresponding Office Web App. Figure WEB-2 shows a PowerPoint presentation open in the PowerPoint Web App. You can also use an Office Web App to create a new file, which is saved automatically to SkyDrive while you work. In addition, you can download a file created with an Office Web App and continue to work with the file in the full version of the corresponding Office application: Word, Excel, PowerPoint, or OneNote. Finally, you can create a SkyDrive network that consists of the people you want to be able to view your folders and files on your SkyDrive. You can give people permission to view and edit your files using any computer with an active Internet connection and a Web browser.

FIGURE WEB-1: SkyDrive on Windows Live

Browser window

SkyDrive - Windows Live tab

By default, one folder is available on SkyDrive; you can create additional folders

The name of the person who signed into Windows Live and SkyDrive appears here

Monitors the amount of space still available on your SkyDrive

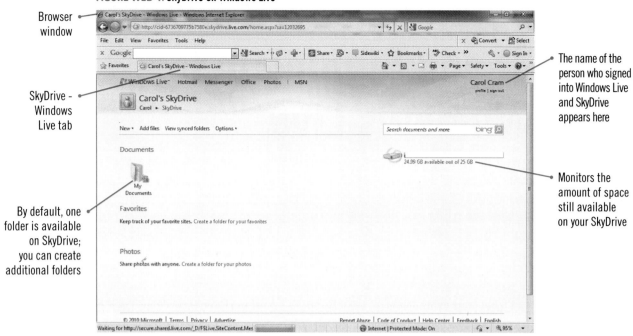

FIGURE WEB-2: PowerPoint presentation open in the PowerPoint Web App

Browser window

Ribbon available in PowerPoint Web App

The presentation in PowerPoint Web App maintains the same look and feel as the same presentation in the desktop version of PowerPoint

Name of PowerPoint presentation open in PowerPoint Web App

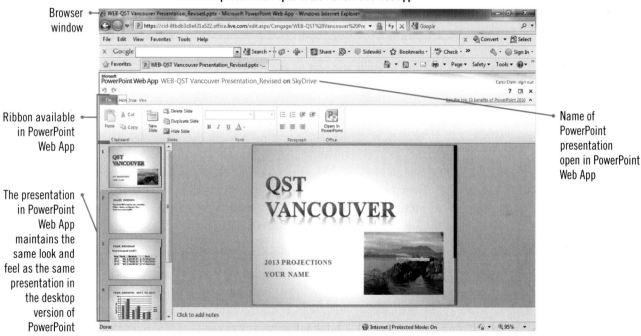

TABLE WEB-1: Services available via Windows Live

service	description
E-mail	Send and receive e-mail using a Hotmail account
Instant Messaging	Use Messenger to chat with friends, share photos, and play games
SkyDrive	Store files, work on files using Office Web Apps, and share files with people in your network
Photos	Upload and share photos with friends
People	Develop a network of friends and coworkers, then use the network to distribute information and stay in touch
Downloads	Access a variety of free programs available for download to a PC
Mobile Device	Access applications for a mobile device: text messaging, using Hotmail, networking, and sharing photos

Obtaining a Windows Live ID and Signing In to Windows Live

To work with your files online using SkyDrive and Office Web Apps, you need a Windows Live ID. You obtain a Windows Live ID by going to the Windows Live Web site and creating a new account. Once you have a Windows Live ID, you can access SkyDrive and then use it to store your files, create new files, and share your files with friends and coworkers. Mary Lou Jacobs, your supervisor at QST Vancouver, asks you to obtain a Windows Live ID so that you can work on documents with your coworkers. You go to the Windows Live Web site, create a Windows Live ID, and then sign in to your SkyDrive.

STEPS

QUICK TIP

If you already have a Windows Live ID, go to the next lesson and sign in as directed using your account.

1. **Open your Web browser, type home.live.com in the Address bar, then press [Enter]**

   The Windows Live home page opens. From this page, you can create a Windows Live account and receive your Windows Live ID.

2. **Click the Sign up button** *(Note: You may see a Sign up link instead of a button)*

   The Create your Windows Live ID page opens.

3. **Click the Or use your own e-mail address link under the Check availability button or if you are already using Hotmail, Messenger, or Xbox LIVE, click the Sign in now link in the Information statement near the top of the page**

4. **Enter the information required, as shown in Figure WEB-3**

   If you wish, you can sign up for a Windows Live e-mail address such as yourname@live.com so that you can also access the Windows Live e-mail services.

TROUBLE

The code can be difficult to read. If you receive an error message, enter the new code that appears.

5. **Enter the code shown at the bottom of your screen, then click the I accept button**

   The Windows Live home page opens. The name you entered when you signed up for your Windows Live ID appears in the top right corner of the window to indicate that you are signed in to Windows Live. From the Windows Live home page, you can access all the services and applications offered by Windows Live. See the Verifying your Windows Live ID box for information on finalizing your account set up.

6. **Point to Windows Live, as shown in Figure WEB-4**

   A list of options appears. SkyDrive is one of the options you can access directly from Windows Live.

TROUBLE

Click I accept if you are asked to review and accept the Windows Live Service Agreement and Privacy Statement.

7. **Click SkyDrive**

   The SkyDrive page opens. Your name appears in the top right corner, and the amount of space available is shown on the right side of the SkyDrive page. The amount of space available is monitored, as indicated by the gauge that fills with color as space is used. Using SkyDrive, you can add files to the existing folder and you can create new folders.

8. **Click sign out in the top right corner under your name, then exit the Web browser**

   You are signed out of your Windows Live account. You can sign in again directly from the Windows Live page in your browser or from within a file created with PowerPoint, Excel, Word, or OneNote.

FIGURE WEB-3: Creating a Windows Live ID

Click to sign in using a Hotmail, Messenger, or Xbox Live account

Once your registration is complete, you will be asked to verify your ID

A different code will appear on your screen

Type your e-mail address

You can choose to get a Windows Live e-mail address

Enter the information required

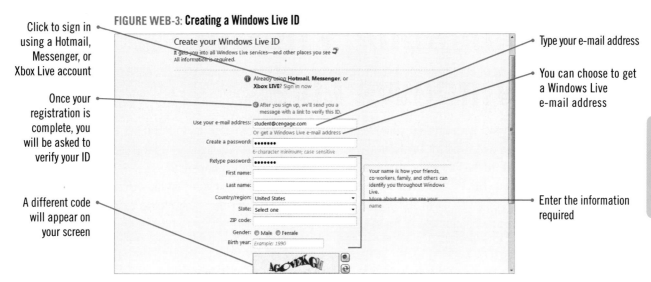

FIGURE WEB-4: Selecting SkyDrive

SkyDrive in the list of Windows Live options

Information about your Windows Live network

Your name appears here

Click to quickly add people to your network

An advertisement appropriate for your location appears here

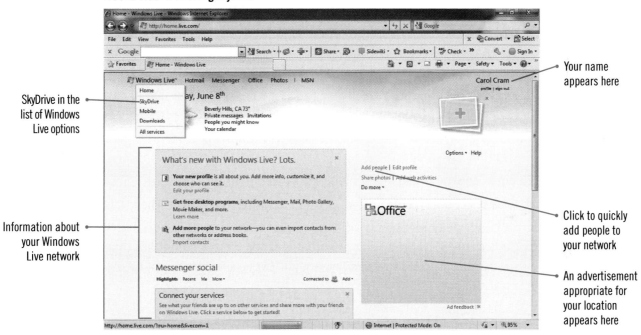

Verifying your Windows Live ID

As soon as you accept the Windows Live terms, an e-mail is sent to the e-mail address you supplied when you created your Windows Live ID. Open your e-mail program, and then open the e-mail from Microsoft with the Subject line: Confirm your e-mail address for Windows Live. Follow the simple, step-by-step instructions in the e-mail to confirm your Windows Live ID. When the confirmation is complete, you will be asked to sign in to Windows Live, using your e-mail address and password. Once signed in, you will see your Windows Live Account page.

Uploading Files to Windows Live

Once you have created your Windows Live ID, you can sign in to Windows Live directly from Word, PowerPoint, Excel, or OneNote and start saving and uploading files. You upload files to your SkyDrive so you can share the files with other people, access the files from another computer, or use SkyDrive's additional storage.  You open a PowerPoint presentation, access your Windows Live account from Backstage view, and save a file to SkyDrive on Windows Live. You also create a new folder called Cengage directly from Backstage view and add a file to it.

STEPS

1. **Start PowerPoint, open the file** WEB-1.pptx **from the drive and folder where you store your Data Files, then save the file as** WEB-QST Vancouver Presentation

2. **Click the** File **tab, then click** Save & Send
   The Save & Send options available in PowerPoint are listed in Backstage view, as shown in Figure WEB-5.

3. **Click** Save to Web

QUICK TIP
Skip this step if the computer you are using signs you in automatically.

4. **Click** Sign In, **type your e-mail address, press** [Tab], **type your** password, **then click** OK
   The My Documents folder on your SkyDrive appears in the Save to Windows Live SkyDrive information area.

5. **Click** Save As, **wait a few seconds for the Save As dialog box to appear, then click** Save
   The file is saved to the My Documents folder on the SkyDrive that is associated with your Windows Live account. You can also create a new folder and upload files directly to SkyDrive from your hard drive.

6. **Click the** File **tab, click** Save & Send, **click** Save to Web, **then sign in if the My Documents folder does not automatically appear in Backstage view**

7. **Click the** New Folder **button in the Save to Windows Live SkyDrive pane, then sign in to Windows Live if directed**

8. **Type** Cengage **as the folder name, click** Next, **then click** Add files

9. **Click** select documents from your computer, **then navigate to the location on your computer where you saved the file WEB-QST Vancouver Presentation in Step 1**

10. **Click** WEB-QST Vancouver Presentation.pptx **to select it, then click** Open
    You can continue to add more files; however, you have no more files to upload at this time.

11. **Click** Continue
    In a few moments, the PowerPoint presentation is uploaded to your SkyDrive, as shown in Figure WEB-6. You can simply store the file on SkyDrive or you can choose to work on the presentation using the PowerPoint Web App.

12. **Click the** PowerPoint icon 🖼 **on your taskbar to return to PowerPoint, then close the presentation and exit PowerPoint**

FIGURE WEB-5: Save & Send options in Backstage view

PowerPoint file

Save & Send area
in Backstage view

Save to Web
option

FIGURE WEB-6: File uploaded to the Cengage folder on Windows Live

Browser
window

Path to file

Current folder
menu bar

Uploaded file

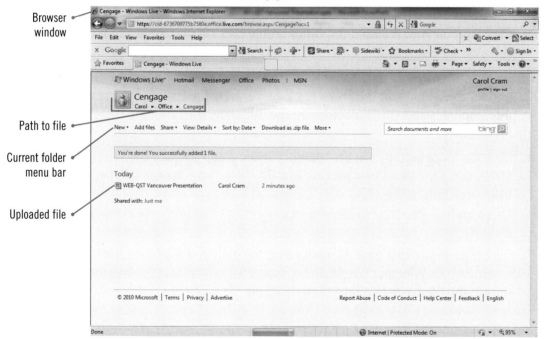

Working with the PowerPoint Web App

Once you have uploaded a file to SkyDrive on Windows Live, you can work on it using its corresponding Office Web App. **Office Web Apps** provide you with the tools you need to view documents online and to edit them right in your browser. You do not need to have Office programs installed on the computer you use to access SkyDrive and Office Web Apps. From SkyDrive, you can also open the document directly in the full Office application (for example, PowerPoint) if the application is installed on the computer you are using. ▓▓▓▓▓ You use the PowerPoint Web App to make some edits to the PowerPoint presentation. You then open the presentation in PowerPoint and use the full version to make additional edits.

STEPS

TROUBLE

Click the browser button on the taskbar, then click the Windows Live SkyDrive window to make it the active window.

1. **Click the WEB-QST Vancouver Presentation file in the Cengage folder on SkyDrive**

   The presentation opens in your browser window. A menu is available, which includes the options you have for working with the file.

2. **Click Edit in Browser, then if a message appears related to installing the Sign-in Assistant, click the Close button ✖ to the far right of the message**

   In a few moments, the PowerPoint presentation opens in the PowerPoint Web App, as shown in Figure WEB-7. Table WEB-2 lists the commands you can perform using the PowerPoint Web App.

QUICK TIP

The changes you make to the presentation are saved automatically on SkyDrive.

3. **Enter your name where indicated on Slide 1, click Slide 3 (New Tours) in the Slides pane, then click Delete Slide in the Slides group**

   The slide is removed from the presentation. You decide to open the file in the full version of PowerPoint on your computer so you can apply WordArt to the slide title. You work with the file in the full version of PowerPoint when you want to use functions, such as WordArt, that are not available on the PowerPoint Web App.

4. **Click Open in PowerPoint in the Office group, click OK in response to the message, then click Allow if requested**

   In a few moments, the revised version of the PowerPoint slide opens in PowerPoint on your computer.

5. **Click Enable Editing on the Protected View bar near the top of your presentation window if prompted, select QST Vancouver on the title slide, then click the Drawing Tools Format tab**

QUICK TIP

Use the ScreenTips to help you find the required WordArt style.

6. **Click the More button ▼ in the WordArt Styles group to show the selection of WordArt styles, select the WordArt style Gradient Fill - Blue-Gray, Accent 4, Reflection, then click a blank area outside the slide**

   The presentation appears in PowerPoint as shown in Figure WEB-8. Next, you save the revised version of the file to SkyDrive.

7. **Click the File tab, click Save As, notice that the path in the Address bar is to the Cengage folder on your Windows Live SkyDrive, type WEB-QST Vancouver Presentation_Revised. pptx in the File name text box, then click Save**

   The file is saved to your SkyDrive.

TROUBLE

The browser opens to the Cengage folder but the file is not visible. Follow Step 8 to open the Cengage folder and refresh the list of files in the folder.

8. **Click the browser icon on the taskbar to open your SkyDrive page, then click Office next to your name in the SkyDrive path, view a list of recent documents, then click Cengage in the list to the left of the recent documents list to open the Cengage folder**

   Two PowerPoint files now appear in the Cengage folder.

9. **Exit the Web browser and close all tabs if prompted, then exit PowerPoint**

FIGURE WEB-7: Presentation opened in the PowerPoint Web App from Windows Live

Browser window

Name of Web App

PowerPoint Web App Ribbon

URL is the file location

FIGURE WEB-8: Revised PowerPoint presentation

PowerPoint title bar

PowerPoint Ribbon

Presentation title enhanced using full version of PowerPoint

Name added using PowerPoint Web App

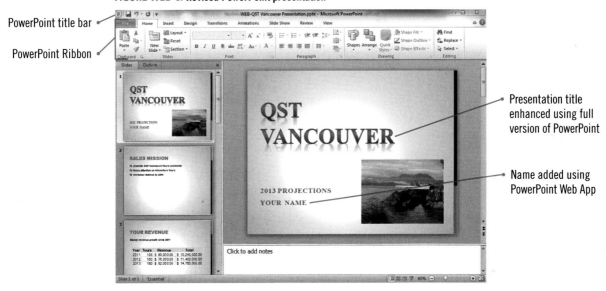

TABLE WEB-2: Commands on the PowerPoint Web App

tab	commands available
File	• Open in PowerPoint: select to open the file in PowerPoint on your computer • Where's the Save Button?: when you click this option, a message appears telling you that you do not need to save your presentation when you are working on it with PowerPoint Web App. The presentation is saved automatically as you work. • Print • Share • Properties • Give Feedback • Privacy • Terms of Use • Close
Home	• Clipboard group: Cut, Copy, Paste • Slides group: Add a New Slide, Delete a Slide, Duplicate a Slide, and Hide a Slide • Font group: Work with text: change the font, style, color, and size of selected text • Paragraph group: Work with paragraphs: add bullets and numbers, indent text, align text • Office group: Open the file in PowerPoint on your computer
Insert	• Insert a Picture • Insert a SmartArt diagram • Insert a link such as a link to another file on SkyDrive or to a Web page
View	• Editing view (the default) • Reading view • Slide Show view • Notes view

Creating Folders and Organizing Files on SkyDrive

As you have learned, you can sign in to SkyDrive directly from the Office applications PowerPoint, Excel, Word, and OneNote, or you can access SkyDrive directly through your Web browser. This option is useful when you are away from the computer on which you normally work or when you are using a computer that does not have Office applications installed. You can go to SkyDrive, create and organize folders, and then create or open files to work on with Office Web Apps. You access SkyDrive from your Web browser, create a new folder called Illustrated, and delete one of the PowerPoint files from the My Documents folder.

STEPS

TROUBLE
Go to Step 3 if you are already signed in.

1. **Open your Web browser, type home.live.com in the Address bar, then press [Enter]**
   The Windows Live home page opens. From here, you can sign in to your Windows Live account and then access SkyDrive.

TROUBLE
Type your Windows Live ID (your e-mail) and password, then click Sign in if prompted to do so.

2. **Sign into Windows Live as directed**
   You are signed in to your Windows Live page. From this page, you can take advantage of the many applications available on Windows Live, including SkyDrive.

3. **Point to Windows Live, then click SkyDrive**
   SkyDrive opens.

4. **Click Cengage, then point to WEB-QST Vancouver Presentation.pptx**
   A menu of options for working with the file, including a Delete button to the far right, appears to the right of the filename.

5. **Click the Delete button ⊠, then click OK**
   The file is removed from the Cengage folder on your SkyDrive. You still have a copy of the file on your computer.

6. **Point to Windows Live, then click SkyDrive**
   Your SkyDrive screen with the current selection of folders available on your SkyDrive opens, as shown in Figure WEB-9.

7. **Click New, click Folder, type Illustrated, click Next, click Office in the path under Add documents to Illustrated at the top of the window, then click View all in the list under Personal**
   You are returned to your list of folders, where you see the new Illustrated folder.

8. **Click Cengage, point to WEB-QST Vancouver Presentation_Revised.pptx, click More, click Move, then click the Illustrated folder**

9. **Click Move this file into Illustrated, as shown in Figure WEB-10**
   The file is moved to the Illustrated folder.

FIGURE WEB-9: Folders on your SkyDrive

Current location

Folders currently available

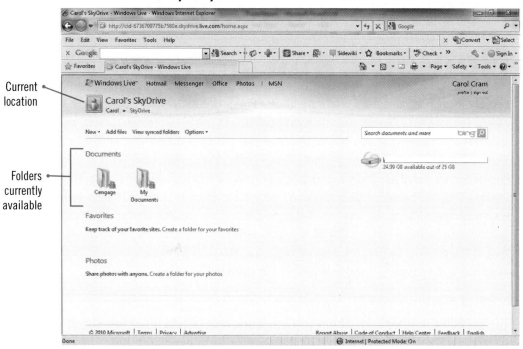

FIGURE WEB-10: Moving a file to the Illustrated folder

Click to move file to this location

Be sure to rename a file before moving it if you are moving it to a location where another copy of the same file exists

Name of file to be moved

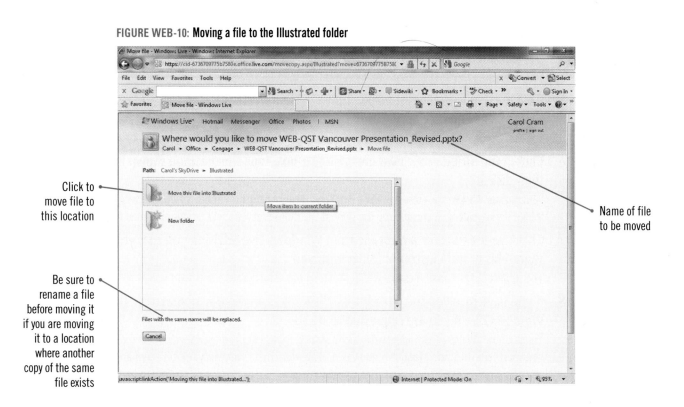

Adding People to Your Network and Sharing Files

One of the great advantages of working with SkyDrive on Windows Live is that you can share your files with others. Suppose, for example, that you want a colleague to review a presentation you created in PowerPoint and then add a new slide. You can, of course, e-mail the presentation directly to your colleague, who can then make changes and e-mail the presentation back. Alternatively, you can save time by uploading the PowerPoint file directly to SkyDrive and then giving your colleague access to the file. Your colleague can edit the file using the PowerPoint Web App, and then you can check the updated file on SkyDrive, also using the PowerPoint Web App. In this way, you and your colleague are working with just one version of the presentation that you both can update. ▓▓▓▓▓ You have decided to share files in the Illustrated folder that you created in the previous lesson with another individual. You start by working with a partner so that you can share files with your partner and your partner can share files with you.

STEPS

1. **Identify a partner with whom you can work, and obtain his or her e-mail address; you can choose someone in your class or someone on your e-mail list, but it should be someone who will be completing these steps when you are**

2. **From the Illustrated folder, click Share**

3. **Click Edit permissions**

   The Edit permissions page opens. On this page, you can select the individual with whom you would like to share the contents of the Illustrated folder.

4. **Click in the Enter a name or an e-mail address text box, type the e-mail address of your partner, then press [Tab]**

   You can define the level of access that you want to give your partner.

5. **Click the Can view files list arrow shown in Figure WEB-11, click Can add, edit details, and delete files, then click Save**

   You can choose to send a notification to each individual when you grant permission to access your files.

6. **Click in the Include your own message text box, type the message shown in Figure WEB-12, then click Send**

   Your partner will receive a message from Windows Live advising him or her that you have shared your Illustrated folder. If your partner is completing the steps at the same time, you will receive an e-mail from your partner.

7. **Check your e-mail for a message from Windows Live advising you that your partner has shared his or her Illustrated folder with you**

   The subject of the e-mail message will be "[Name] has shared documents with you."

8. **If you have received the e-mail, click View folder in the e-mail message, then sign in to Windows Live if you are requested to do so**

   You are now able to access your partner's Illustrated folder on his or her SkyDrive. You can download files in your partner's Illustrated folder to your own computer where you can work on them and then upload them again to your partner's Illustrated shared folder.

9. **Exit the browser**

FIGURE WEB-11: Editing folder permissions

Folder permissions will be changed for the Illustrated folder

Click to select network permission options

Type email address to continue to add people

Person whose permission status will change

Click to select person from list of contacts

Click to select permission option

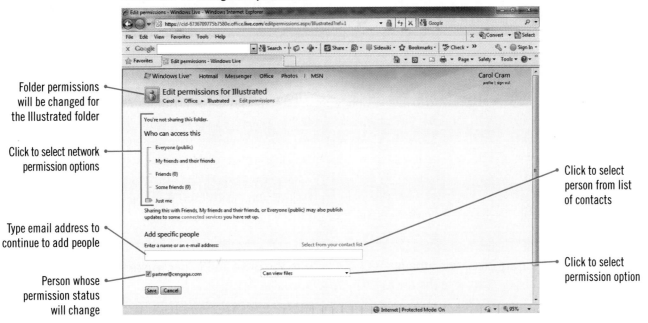

FIGURE WEB-12: Entering a message to notify a person that file sharing permission has been granted

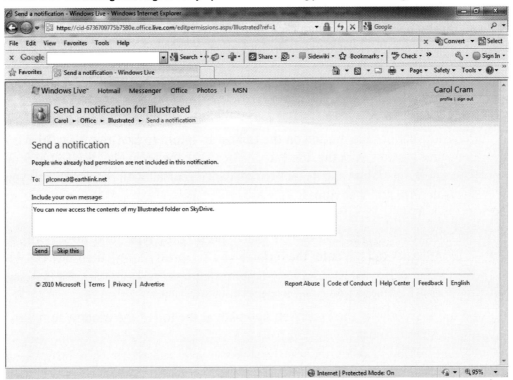

Sharing files on SkyDrive

When you share a folder with other people, the people with whom you share a folder can download the file to their computers and then make changes using the full version of the corresponding Office application.

Once these changes are made, each individual can then upload the file to SkyDrive and into a folder shared with you and others. In this way, you can create a network of people with whom you share your files.

Working with the Excel Web App

You can use the Excel Web App to work with an Excel spreadsheet on SkyDrive. Workbooks opened using the Excel Web App have the same look and feel as workbooks opened using the full version of Excel. However, just like the PowerPoint Web App, the Excel Web App has fewer features available than the full version of Excel. When you want to use a command that is not available on the Excel Web App, you need to open the file in the full version of Excel. You upload an Excel file containing a list of the tours offered by QST Vancouver to the Illustrated folder on SkyDrive. You use the Excel Web App to make some changes, and then you open the revised version in Excel 2010 on your computer.

STEPS

1. **Start Excel, open the file WEB-2.xlsx from the drive and folder where you store your Data Files, then save the file as WEB-QST Vancouver Tours**

   The data in the Excel file is formatted using the Excel table function.

TROUBLE
If prompted, sign in to your Windows Live account as directed.

2. **Click the File tab, click Save & Send, then click Save to Web**

   In a few moments, you should see three folders to which you can save spreadsheets. My Documents and Cengage are personal folder that contains files that only you can access. Illustrated is a shared folder that contains files you can share with others in your network. The Illustrated folder is shared with your partner.

3. **Click the Illustrated folder, click the Save As button, wait a few seconds for the Save As dialog box to appear, then click Save**

QUICK TIP
Alternately, you can open your Web browser and go to Windows Live to sign in to SkyDrive.

4. **Click the File tab, click Save & Send, click Save to Web, click the Windows Live SkyDrive link above your folders, then sign in if prompted**

   Windows Live opens to your SkyDrive.

5. **Click the Excel program button [icon] on the taskbar, then exit Excel**

6. **Click your browser button on the taskbar to return to SkyDrive if SkyDrive is not the active window, click the Illustrated folder, click the Excel file, click Edit in Browser, then review the Ribbon and its tabs to familiarize yourself with the commands you can access from the Excel Web App**

   Table WEB-3 summarizes the commands that are available.

7. **Click cell A12, type Gulf Islands Sailing, press [TAB], type 3000, press [TAB], type 10, press [TAB], click cell D3, enter the formula =B3*C3, press [Enter], then click cell A1**

   The formula is copied automatically to the remaining rows as shown in Figure WEB-13 because the data in the original Excel file was created and formatted as an Excel table.

8. **Click SkyDrive in the Excel Web App path at the top of the window to return to the Illustrated folder**

   The changes you made to the Excel spreadsheet are saved automatically on SkyDrive. You can download the file directly to your computer from SkyDrive.

9. **Point to the Excel file, click More, click Download, click Save, navigate to the location where you save the files for this book, name the file WEB-QST Vancouver Tours_Updated, click Save, then click Close in the Download complete dialog box**

   The updated version of the spreadsheet is saved on your computer and on SkyDrive.

10. **Exit the Web browser**

FIGURE WEB-13: Updated table in the Excel Web App

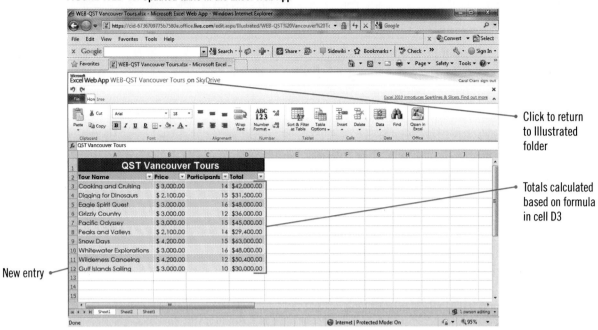

Click to return to Illustrated folder

Totals calculated based on formula in cell D3

New entry

TABLE WEB-3: Commands on the Excel Web App

tab	commands available
File	• Open in Excel: select to open the file in Excel on your computer • Where's the Save Button?: when you click this option, a message appears telling you that you do not need to save your spreadsheet when you are working in it with Excel Web App; the spreadsheet is saved automatically as you work • Save As • Share • Download a Snapshot: a snapshot contains only the values and the formatting; you cannot modify a snapshot • Download a Copy: the file can be opened and edited in the full version of Excel • Give Feedback • Privacy Statement • Terms of Use • Close
Home	• Clipboard group: Cut, Copy, Paste • Font group: change the font, style, color, and size of selected labels and values, as well as border styles and fill colors • Alignment group: change vertical and horizontal alignment and turn on the Wrap Text feature • Number group: change the number format and increase or decrease decimal places • Tables: sort and filter data in a table and modify Table Options • Cells: insert and delete cells • Data: refresh data and find labels or values • Office: open the file in Excel on your computer
Insert	• Insert a Table • Insert a Hyperlink to a Web page

Exploring other Office Web Apps

Two other Office Web Apps are Word and OneNote. You can share files on SkyDrive directly from Word or from OneNote using the same method you used to share files from PowerPoint and Excel. After you upload a Word or OneNote file to SkyDrive, you can work with it in its corresponding Office Web App. To familiarize yourself with the commands available in an Office Web App, open the file and then review the commands on each tab on the Ribbon. If you want to perform a task that is not available in the Office Web App, open the file in the full version of the application.

In addition to working with uploaded files, you can create files from new on SkyDrive. Simply sign in to SkyDrive and open a folder. With a folder open, click New and then select the Web App you want to use to create the new file.

Windows Live and Microsoft Office Web Apps Quick Reference

To Do This	Go Here
Access Windows Live	From the Web browser, type **home.live.com**, then click Sign In
Access SkyDrive on Windows Live	From the Windows Live home page, point to Windows Live, then click SkyDrive
Save to Windows Live from Word, PowerPoint, or Excel	File tab | Save & Send | Save to Web | Select a folder | Save As
Create a New Folder from Backstage view	File tab | Save & Send | Save to Web | New Folder button
Edit a File with a Web App	From SkyDrive, click the file, then click Edit in Browser
Open a File in a desktop version of the application from a Web App: Word, Excel, PowerPoint	Click Open in [Application] in the Office group in each Office Web App
Share files on Windows Live	From SkyDrive, click the folder containing the files to share, click Share on the menu bar, click Edit permissions, enter the e-mail address of the person to share files with, click the Can view files list arrow, click Can add, edit details, and delete files, then click Save

Glossary

Active The currently available document, program, or object; on the taskbar, the button of the active document appears in a darker shade while the buttons of other open documents are dimmed.

Address book A stored list of names and e-mail addresses that you can access through an e-mail program such as Outlook to address messages.

Account Log-on information including ISP, E-mail address and password for each person using Outlook; used to create folders in Outlook for contacts, e-mail and schedules.

Appointment In the Calendar in Outlook, an activity that does not involve inviting other people or scheduling resources.

Attachment A file, such as a picture, audio clip, video clip, document, worksheet, or presentation, that is sent in addition to the e-mail message composed by typing in the Message window.

Backward-compatible Software feature that enables documents saved in an older version of a program to be opened in a newer version of the program.

Blind courtesy copy (BCC) In e-mail, a way to send a message to a recipient who needs to be aware of the correspondence between the sender and the recipients, but is not the primary recipient of the message, and is used when the sender does not want to reveal who has received courtesy copies.

Calendar In Microsoft Outlook, provides a convenient way to manage your appointments and events.

Categories In Outlook, a feature used to tag items so you can track and organize them by specific criteria.

Clipboard Temporary storage area in Windows.

Cloud computing When data, applications, and resources are stored on servers accessed over the Internet or a company's internal network rather than on users' computers.

Commercial provider A company that typically provides electronic services such cable, TV, voice, e-mail, and data communications, as well as Web space, such as America Online.

Compatible The capability of different programs to work together and exchange data.

Computer network The hardware and software that make it possible for two or more computers to share information and resources.

Contacts In Microsoft Outlook, enables you to manage all your business and personal contact information.

Contact Group A named subset of the people in your Outlook Contacts folder, grouped together by e-mail addresses.

Contextual tab Tab with grouped commands on the Ribbon that appears when needed to complete a specific task; for example, if you insert an picture as you compose a message, the contextual Picture Tools Format tab appears with buttons you can use the adjust, change, or resize the picture.

Courtesy copy (CC) In e-mail, a way to send a message to a recipient who needs to be aware of the correspondence between the sender and the recipients, but is not the primary recipient of the message.

Date Navigator A monthly calendar in the To-Do Bar that gives you an overview of the month.

Deleted Items folder The folder that stores items when you delete or erase a message from any mail folder, rather than being immediately, permanently deleted. Also called trash folder.

Dialog box launcher An icon available in many groups on the Ribbon that you can click to open a dialog box or task pane, offering an alternative way to choose commands.

Distribution list A collection of contacts to whom you want to send the same messages; makes it possible for you to send a message to the same group without having to select each contact in the group. *See also* Contact Group.

Document window Workspace in the program window that displays the current document.

Drafts folder Stores unfinished messages that you can finish writing at a later time. Many programs automatically save unsent messages at regular intervals in the drafts folder as a safety measure.

Electronic mail (e-mail) The technology that makes it possible for you to send and receive messages through the Internet.

E-mail message A message sent using e-mail technology.

E-mail software Enables you to send and receive e-mail messages over a network, within an intranet, and through the Internet.

Emoticon A symbol created by combining keyboard characters; used to communicate feelings in e-mails.

Event In the Calendar in Outlook, an activity that lasts 24 hours or longer.

Field In an Outlook contact, an area that stores one piece of information, such as a first name or an e-mail address.

File An electronic collection of stored data that has a unique name, distinguishing it from other files.

Filter Used to create a subset of a list, you search for only specific information—for example, in Outlook Contacts, filter only for those contacts who live in New Jersey.

Flag In many e-mail programs such as Microsoft Outlook, a method of coding the messages by assigning different colored flags to messages to categorize them or indicate their level of importance for followup.

Forwarding Sending an e-mail message you have received to someone else.

Gallery A collection of choices you can browse through to make a selection. Often available with Live Preview.

Group On the Ribbon, a set of related commands on a tab.

Inbox A mail folder that stores all incoming mail.

Integrate To incorporate a document and parts of a document created in one program into another program; for example, to incorporate an Excel chart into a PowerPoint slide, or an Access table into a Word document.

Interface The look and feel of a program; for example, the appearance of commands and the way they are organized in the program window.

Internet A network of connected computers and computer networks located around the world.

Internet Service Provider (ISP) A company that maintains Internet computers and telecommunications equipment in order to provide Internet access to businesses, organizations, and ¬individuals.

Intranet A computer network that connects computers in a local area only, such as computers in a company's office.

Journal In Outlook, provides a trail of your activities within Microsoft Office by tracking all documents, spreadsheets, databases, presentations, or any Office file that you specify. When turned on, you can see a timeline of any calls, messages, appointments, or tasks.

Junk e-mail Unwanted mail that arrives from unsolicited sources. Also called spam.

Label In some e-mail programs, the ability to assign an indicator to an e-mail message to help sort or organize your e-mail messages.

Launch To open or start a program on your computer.

Live Preview A feature that lets you point to a choice in a gallery or palette and see the results in the document without actually clicking the choice.

MapIt An Outlook feature on a Contact card that lets you view a contact's address on a map.

Meeting In the Calendar in Outlook, an activity you invite people to or reserve resources for.

Message body In an e-mail message, where you write the text of your message.

Message header Contains the basic information about a message including the sender's name and e-mail address, the names and e-mail addresses of recipients and CC recipients, a date and time stamp, and the subject of the message.

Navigation Pane In Outlook in Normal view, it is typically on the left side of the screen, showing you the folder list in addition to the navigation shortcuts.

Notes In Outlook, the electronic version of the sticky notes or Post-It™ notes you buy at your local stationery store; a convenient way to quickly jot down a reminder or an idea.

Office Web App Versions of the Microsoft Office applications with limited functionality that are available online from Windows Live SkyDrive. Users can view documents online and then edit them in the browser using a selection of functions. Office Web Apps are available for Word, PowerPoint, Excel, and One Note

Online collaboration The ability to incorporate feedback or share information across the Internet or a company network or intranet.

Outbox A temporary storage folder for e-mail messages that have not yet been sent.

Outlook Today Shows your day at a glance, like an electronic version of a daily planner book. When it is open, you can see what is happening in the Calendar, Tasks, and Messages for the day.

Personal account In Outlook, identifies you as a user with information such as your e-mail address and password, the type of Internet service provider (ISP) you are using, and the incoming and outgoing mail server address for your ISP.

Previewing Prior to printing, to see onscreen exactly how the printed document will look.

Program tab Single tab on the Ribbon specific to a particular view, such as Print Preview.

Quick Access toolbar Customizable toolbar that includes buttons for common Office commands, such as saving a file and undoing an action.

Really Simple Syndication (RSS) A format for feeding or syndicating news or any content from Web sites to your computer.

Ribbon Area that displays commands for the current Office program, organized into tabs and groups.

Rule In Outlook, enables you to organize your mail, by setting parameters for incoming mail. For example, you can specify that all mail from a certain person goes into the folder for a specific project.

Screen capture A snapshot of your screen, as if you took a picture of it with a camera, which you can paste into a document.

Sent Items folder When you send an e-mail message, a copy of the message is stored in this folder to help you track the messages you send out.

Service provider The organization or company that provides e-mail or Internet access. See also Internet Service Provider.

SkyDrive An online storage and file sharing service. Access to SkyDrive is through a Windows Live account. Up to 25 GB of data can be stored in a personal SkyDrive, with each file a maximum size of 50 MB.

Sort To reorder e-mail message information, such as by date.

Spam Unwanted mail that arrives from unsolicited sources. Also called junk e-mail.

Spamming The sending of identical or near-identical unsolicited messages to a large number of recipients. Many e-mail programs have filters that identify this mail and place it in a special folder.

Store-and-forward technology Messages are *stored* on a service provider's computer until a recipient logs on to a computer and requests his or her messages. At that time, the messages are *forwarded* to the recipient's computer.

Suite A group of programs that are bundled together and share a similar interface, making it easy to transfer skills and program content among them.

Tab A set of commands on the Ribbon related to a common set of tasks or features. Tabs are further organized into groups of related commands.

Tasks In Outlook, the electronic to-do list, whereby each task has a subject, a start and end date, priority, and a description.

Themes Predesigned combinations of colors, fonts, and formatting attributes you can apply to a document in any Office program.

Threaded message Includes all e-mails that discuss a common subject. Message threading allows you to navigate through a group of messages, seeing all replies and forwards from all recipients

Title bar Area at the top of every program window that displays the document and program name.

Trash folder *See* Deleted Items folder.

Username The first part of an e-mail address that identifies the person who receives the mail that is sent to this e-mail address.

User interface A collective term for all the ways you interact with a software program.

Vacation response An automatically-generated e-mail you can have sent in response to received e-mails when you are away; most e-mail programs allow you to create a vacation response.

Views Display settings that show or hide selected elements of a document in the document window, to make it easier to focus on a certain task, such as formatting or reading text.

Web-based e-mail Web site that provides free e-mail addresses and service.

Windows Live A collection of services and Web applications that people can access through a login. Windows Live services include access to e-mail and instant messaging, storage of files on SkyDrive, sharing and storage of photos, networking with people, downloading software, and interfacing with a mobile device.

XML Acronym that stands for eXtensible Markup Language, which is a language used to structure, store, and send information.

Zooming in A feature that makes a document appear larger but shows less of it onscreen at once; does not affect actual document size.

Zooming out A feature that shows more of a document onscreen at once but at a reduced size; does not affect actual document size.

Index